EMPATHS AND NARCISSISTS

2 IN 1 BUNDLE

JUDY DYER

EMPATHS AND NARCISSISTS: 2 in 1 Bundle
by Judy Dyer

© **Copyright 2020 by Judy Dyer**

All Rights Reserved.

Disclaimer: This book is designed to provide accurate and authoritative information in regard to the subject matter covered. By its sale, neither the publisher nor the author is engaged in rendering psychological or other professional services. If expert assistance or counseling is needed, the services of a competent professional should be sought.

ISBN: 979-8662975033

ALSO BY JUDY DYER

Empath: A Complete Guide for Developing Your Gift and Finding Your Sense of Self

The Highly Sensitive: How to Stop Emotional Overload, Relieve Anxiety, and Eliminate Negative Energy

Empath and The Highly Sensitive: 2 in 1 Bundle

Anger Management: How to Take Control of Your Emotions and Find Joy in Life

Borderline Personality Disorder: A Complete BPD Guide for Managing Your Emotions and Improving Your Relationships

THE EMPOWERED EMPATH

A SIMPLE SURVIVAL GUIDE ON SETTING
BOUNDARIES, CONTROLLING YOUR EMOTIONS,
AND MAKING LIFE EASIER

BY: JUDY DYER

CONTENTS

INTRODUCTION

E mpaths feel the emotions of others, from joy to pain and everything in between. They find it impossible to be in the presence of another person and not feel what they feel. Human beings want to be happy and spend the majority of their lives chasing that which they feel will complete them and bring them fulfillment. Unfortunately, most people don't find happiness—they hate their jobs, they feel trapped in unloving relationships, they feel insecure, and they want more out of life. These unfulfilled wants, needs, and desires cause sadness and depression, and people carry these feelings of heaviness every day. Unfortunately for the empath, not only do they have to deal with their own demons, but their natural ability to tune into the feelings of others forces them to deal with the demons of those they come into contact with. It is only natural to want to fight against this; after all, who wants to feel sad all the time, especially when that sadness does not belong to you?

In an attempt to stop this pain, empaths build defense mechanisms around them that prevent them from enjoying life. Despite the fortress they attempt to shield themselves with, they still absorb negative energy in the form of pain, suffering, and even illness, causing them to spend much of their lives feeling scared, sick, and lonely. Considering all that empaths are forced to endure, it is no wonder some of them are afraid to embrace their gift. However, learning how to use empathic abilities as a blessing and not a curse is essential to healthy living. Empathy is not something you can escape from—you either embrace it and use it the way it was intended or live a life of misery and suffering. You are the only person who can make that decision.

Think about a child who is naturally talented at playing the piano. When he hears music, he is able to replay it exactly as he heard it. This is his gift. He didn't learn how to play the piano, it just comes naturally to him. But if the child wants to master his craft, he is going to have to study music. If he wants to become a concert pianist, he will need to study interpersonal dynamics and practice with a group. Good teaching will accelerate his skills and enable him to become a brilliant performer or teacher. But to learn, he will need to connect with people.

In a similar fashion, empaths need to learn skills that will enhance their gift. They can shy away from this and operate on a low level, or they can enhance it and become exceptional. Empathic abilities when ignored, misused, or misunderstood can lead you into a dark place. You become weak, drained, and lifeless, burdened with responsibilities that don't belong to you, and you suffer unnecessary illness. Inasmuch as empaths have a desire to help people, taking on other people's burdens will not only hinder you but also hinder the person you are trying to help. Would you want a friend or loved one carrying your burdens? I am assuming that one hundred percent of you would answer no to this question. So, the question then becomes, if you don't want someone else carrying your burdens, why would you want to carry someone else's?

In my first book, *Empath: A Complete Guide for Developing Your Gift and Finding Your Sense of Self,* I shared with you how to recognize that you have a gift and how to tap into it; but due to popular demand, I want to answer some questions that will further help you enhance your gift and become all you were called to be.

I don't believe in coincidences. I believe in divine appointments, and you are exactly where you need to be because you are ready to step into a new level of empowerment and clarity that is going to launch you into your destiny.

In order to maximize the value you receive from this book, I highly encourage you to join our tight-knit community on Facebook. Here you will be able to connect and share with other like-minded Empaths to continue your growth.

Taking this journey alone is not recommended, and this can be an excellent support network for you.

It would be great to connect with you there,

Judy Dyer

To Join, Visit: www.pristinepublish.com/empathgroup

DOWNLOAD THE AUDIO VERSION OF THIS BOOK FREE

If you love listening to audiobooks on-the-go or would enjoy a narration as you read along, I have great news for you. You can download the audiobook version of Empaths and Narcissists for FREE (Regularly $19.95) just by signing up for a FREE 30-day audible trial!

Visit: www.pristinepublish.com/audiobooks

CHAPTER 1:

UNDERSTANDING ENERGY

E mpaths have a better understanding of energy than they do the words that are coming out of a person's mouth. This is one of the reasons you can't lie to an empath—they will sense it. Empaths can listen to someone speaking a language they don't understand but have full insight into what they are trying to express based on their energy. Empaths listen to words, pay attention to body language, and translate energetic vibrations. They are especially vulnerable to negativity because it takes from their energy field. On the other hand, when empaths are surrounded by positive energy, they become relaxed and their aura expands in an outward direction as their feelings and emotions flow freely without tension. Positive energy is like a charger—it boosts you up and refills you. This is why empaths will avoid conflict at all costs, shut down when confronted with it, and stay away from certain people and places. The body goes into self-defense mode in an attempt to preserve energy so that you don't become tired and exhausted.

Whether you know it or not, empaths can choose who and what influences their energy—they decide where it is sent and to whom. Our thoughts are so powerful that as soon as they are released, anyone capable of tuning in to your frequency will automatically pick them up. In other words, empaths have the ability to read minds. A skilled empath knows how to protect themselves by being fully aware of what is taking place around them and being present so that no one is able to enter their energy field without their permission.

Once you learn how energy works, it is important that you use it wisely. Remember what goes around comes around, and whatever you put out into the world will come right back to you. Energy is like a drug—the more you experiment with it and enjoy the way it makes you feel, the easier it is to become addicted to it. Your energy, if not protected, will abandon you, become reckless, and attach itself to any other energy circulating in the atmosphere. When empaths are alert and aware, they can quickly recognize subtle changes that take place in their environment without needing to use any of their five senses—smell, touch, taste, sight, or hearing.

Once energy has been released, it travels in an outward direction and never dies. It remains in the air and clings to people or objects, and other energies absorb it or connect with it. Our energy leaves a legacy wherever we go, which is why you can step into an environment and immediately pick up on the vibe of it. That vibe is dependent upon the people or the event that is taking place there.

Once you realize that your energy is constantly interacting with other people's energy, regardless of space, time, or distance, it can become overwhelming, and you will feel as though you need to get back to yourself. But this is because society has conditioned us to believe that our mind and body are two separate entities.

Empaths have a deep desire to discover who they are and what they were put on this earth to do. The awakening process is an extremely traumatic and painful one, parallel to the metamorphosis of the caterpillar into a butterfly. It is a dark and lonely time, but once you discover your truth, you will emerge like a beautiful butterfly and soar to new heights. It is during this time that you come to the revelation that we are not separate or individual but a part of something tremendous—energy and the universe.

You are not always going to be able to explain your gift because there are some aspects of it that are illogical, and in a world that relies on logic, mathematics, and scientific studies, this can be difficult to comprehend. Empaths feel and sense their way through life. They do not need men in white coats to explain what they inherently know about their natural existence. People who don't understand the gift will chalk it up to whatever their imaginations can conjure up and refuse to believe that such a thing exists. Such people are afraid to challenge the status quo and think outside the box; they are afraid of the unknown. They are confined by what they can see with their natural eyes, and if they can't see it, they won't believe it.

Once you have extensive knowledge of how energy works, you will immediately discover limitless mind-blowing possibilities. You will realize that your energy never dies and in whatever form it takes, it will continue to exist. When your life is determined by time, you can become disillusioned, especially if you have reached a certain age and not achieved all that you had hoped. When you were 16, you had envisioned that you would be married with kids by the age of 30. But by the age of 35, you still haven't found your soul mate and so you start worrying about how much time you have left to fulfill your dreams. You realize that you have wasted your time slaving away in a job that you don't like, or that you have married the wrong person and allowed your soulmate to slip through your fingers.

In reality, time doesn't exist. The universe has no regard for it. Man created time, and we have structured our lives around it. If time was abolished, there would be mayhem because people wouldn't know what to do with themselves. When we get to a certain age and our bodies start to decay, we assume that time is running out. But even when our bodies have returned to dust, our energy will continue to travel throughout the universe—there is no beginning and no end. We existed before we took residence on earth in a human body, and we will continue to exist when this body disintegrates.

Physically and mentally, empaths are different. Our bodies are porous, so they absorb energy into their muscles, organs, and tissues. This means that you feel other people's pain, distress, suffering, and depression. You can feel every negative emotion even though they don't belong to you, which can have a detrimental effect on your health. On the other hand, you can quickly get in tune with other people's love, happiness, and vitality, which is a fantastic feeling. Empaths feel exhausted when they are surrounded by toxic people, witnessing arguments, violence, and hearing too much noise makes empaths feel physically ill.

Empaths can also feel other people's physical pain and pick up the same symptoms as if they had the illness. This is one of the reasons they find it difficult to work in hospitals. You might find that your mood changes when you get on a bus and sit next to someone who is depressed or anxious. Or you can walk into a store feeling happy or even neutral, but leave feeling tense and exhausted, or even with aches and pains in your body because you have been exposed to the whirlwind of chaos that usually takes place in a store with the bright lights, loud speakers, and crowds of people. There are certain environments that are simply not conducive for empaths.

To survive as an empath, it's crucial to learn how to ground yourself in overstimulating situations and protect yourself against other people's negative energy.

CHAPTER 2:

THE DARK SIDE OF BEING AN EMPATH

There is no doubt that empaths have been blessed with a unique gift; but unfortunately, it can become a curse if you don't understand it and know how to control it. As I am sure you are aware, constantly feeling the stress and pain of others can leave you feeling drained and lifeless. Since your neurological and biological makeup absorbs the emotions of others on a large scale, a lot of empaths experience serious health problems including:

- Headaches
- Back pain
- Digestive issues
- Anxiety
- Chronic depression
- A weak immune system
- Chronic fatigue

On a social level, empaths are extremely compassionate. This trustworthy trait is very appealing to people who are suffering. Unfortunately, many empaths are taken advantage of because of this, and they tend to attract the worst kinds of people—sociopaths, narcissists, and people with a general manipulative character. It has been argued that one of the reasons sociopaths are attracted to empaths is because they don't have any emotions, and so they look to others to fill that void. Empaths are highly emotional people, and sociopaths instinctively know this. They lure the empath in through eye contact, subtle gestures, mannerisms, and body language. Empaths are drawn to this because of their attraction to special feelings.

Empaths find it difficult to make personal choices because they pay so much attention to the emotions of others. They are always worrying about how their decisions might affect the people around them. This leads them to create an image of perfectionism, and there is always a conflict between pleasing others and pleasing themselves. Some empaths want people to think they are perfect, hence their desire to please others, which is a constant struggle (you will learn more about this in chapter 6).

Empaths are very in tune with their instincts, which makes it easy for them to read people immediately. However, being aware of other people's difficulties can become problematic. There is often an overlap between their feelings and the feelings of others, which can have a negative effect on the confidence of an empath. Empaths often find it difficult to understand why they feel the way they do. They often ask themselves, "Am I personally experiencing anxiety or is it coming from someone else?" Some empaths don't know how to handle the emotional overload and will turn to drugs and alcohol as a coping mechanism.

Empaths are often mistaken as being overly sensitive and weak, which can have a negative effect on their self-esteem. Additionally, they find it difficult to watch violent or graphic content and will avoid watching the news or TV in general.

They also feel uncomfortable discussing misfortune, cruelties, and injustices.

Challenges for Empath Males and Females

Male and female empaths experience some of the same, but also different challenges. Empaths are sensitive people—females can show this side of them openly, but males find it difficult because of the social stigma attached to overly emotional men. Boys are raised not to cry, to be strong and macho, and displaying their sensitivities is seen as a sign of weakness. Boys with such characteristics are often bullied at school and labeled as "sissies" and "cry babies." Therefore, empath males find it difficult to talk about how they feel in fear of being judged as not masculine enough. They are not interested in sports like basketball, baseball, and soccer; neither are they interested in aggressive contact sports such as rugby and wrestling, and so they may feel isolated and rejected by their peers. As a result, male empaths tend to repress their emotions and act as if they don't exist. They often suffer in silence feeling that no one understands them, which can have a negative impact on their health, relationships, and careers.

Alanis Morrissette, a known empath, wrote a song entitled "In Praise of the Vulnerable Man." Men must embrace their sensitive nature because it is nothing to be ashamed of. This does not mean being overly feminine, it means being balanced, owning both your masculine and feminine sides. It means being secure enough to be vulnerable and strong enough to be sensitive. Men of this nature have high emotional intelligence. They do not fear their own or other people's emotions, which makes them attractive and compassionate partners, leaders, and friends.

Females, on the other hand, don't experience the same challenges when it comes to emotional sensitivity. Girls are raised to express their emotions—it's okay for them to cry and feel sad. The notion of female intuition is also socially acceptable, but the idea of females being powerful is still frowned upon in Western society. Historically, women have had to and are still fighting for equality. Females have experienced horrendous struggles because of their gender. More than 200 women were arrested and approximately 20 were slaughtered during the Salem witch trials because of their sensitivities.

Even though it is somewhat acceptable, women today are still afraid to express their sensitivities in fear of being judged or misunderstood. This is especially true in relationships because overly emotional women are often deemed as being needy and insecure. It's important that female empaths learn to be authentic in their relationships and openly discuss their needs. They should know how to set boundaries with their time and energy so they don't get overwhelmed and experience burn out. Male or female, an empath who knows how to give and receive in a balanced way holds a lot of power.

CHAPTER 3:

THE DOCTOR CAN'T HELP YOU

E mpaths who don't understand their gift will go and see a health care practitioner for help. They are often misdiagnosed as neurotics, hypochondriacs, or in need of psychiatric assistance for depression or anxiety and prescribed with medication such as Xanax, Valium, or Prozac. This is not what someone dealing with empathetic overload needs. Empaths are also misdiagnosed with Sensory Processing Disorder in which sufferers have difficulty processing sensory stimulation. People with the disorder are said to have an abnormal sensitivity to touch, sound, light, and crowds. Traditional medicine tends to pathologize anything that it doesn't understand.

Unlike alternative medicine, conventional medicine is ignorant about how the human body and energy work together. The body has a distinct energy field, and empaths are extremely sensitive to this. If mainstream medicine is to be of any benefit to highly sensitive people, it needs to gain a thorough understanding of this.

You cannot cure empathy. It is not a medical condition, so prescribing empaths with anti-depressants and anti-anxiety medication is of no use. Empaths simply need to make certain adjustments to their lives, which is what you will learn how to do in the pages of this book. Sometimes, the adjustment is a simple one, and sometimes it is not so simple. For example, Alice went to see her physician because she found it too stressful and experienced severe anxiety when getting on the underground to go to work. Although Alice practiced meditation and other exercises before traveling, it did not relieve her feelings of distress, and so she was prescribed with anti-anxiety medication. She knew she didn't suffer from anxiety because she didn't feel like this all the time, so Alice didn't take the medication and looked for alternative treatment. Her search led her to Juliet, a psychiatrist that happens to be an empath, who suggested that she drive to work instead and avoid rush hour traffic by waking up earlier. Alice was extremely happy with this solution and wondered why she hadn't thought of it herself. She was also reminded that she is a unique individual with unique needs, and she shouldn't feel guilty about being different, which is something that empaths have trouble accepting. You are not like everyone else, and you should stop trying to be. A part of embracing your gift is accepting the fact that you are special. If people can't understand it, that's their problem and not yours. There is no failure in finding ways to cope and deal with your needs, but turning to medication is not one of them.

Now, please note, if you are an empath who has experienced abuse, trauma, or any other type of tragedy, you are going to need psychological help, so please get it. It is also important to mention that due to the highly sensitive nature of an empath when it comes to psychotropic medication, you typically require a lower dosage than everyone else. So, if you do need to take medication, I suggest that you visit an integrative healthcare practitioner who understands subtle energy and will work with you to find the dose that will benefit you the most.

CHAPTER 4:

COPING STRATEGIES: HOW TO COPE WITH BEING AN EMPATH

L iving as an empath is difficult. No one understands your gift, and you feel constantly drained because everyone is pulling on your energy, and the truth is that sometimes you feel as if you are living in a nightmare! The thing is, as I am sure you are well aware, you can't take the gift back to the shop to get a refund—it's yours for life. You can't turn your back on being an empath. It's not the same as a singing gift or an athletic gift where you can just decide that you are not going to sing or play basketball anymore. You have to learn to live a happy and productive life as an empath. So here are some unique coping strategies to help you do this.

EMBRACE YOUR CREATIVE SIDE

Empaths are generally very creative people. They like to draw, paint, and dance, all of which can be very therapeutic. You have a desire to want to save the world from its many troubles, and while this is an admirable goal, the truth is that it's impossible. Expressing yourself through your creativity is a great way to eliminate negative energy and create something beautiful that you can control and be proud of. It is also a way of purging some of the frustration that comes from not being able to heal the planet.

Find something that you are good at, and practice it daily. Incorporate your creativity into your daily routine and you will start to feel less stressed and frustrated about being an empath.

INDEPENDENT LIVING

One of the things that empaths dislike about their gift is that it makes them feel cluttered. They pick up emotions and energy from everywhere, and they want to escape from it all. You are constantly bombarded with stress and negativity, whether it's from people or through the media, and your one desire is to get away.

Empaths find it difficult to separate their true identity from the emotions of others. You are very idealistic and are constantly thinking of ways to improve the lives of others. This strong desire to help people can become compulsive. If you are not an empath and are reading this, you now understand why your friend is so obsessive when it comes to finding solutions to your problems. When listening to a problem, empaths will often come up with an immediate solution and do everything in their power to help fix it. Although this is a good quality to have, it can lead empaths to become emotionally co-dependent because you are constantly relying on the happiness of others to feel satisfied.

The assumption is that there is only one type of co-dependency, which is where a person is emotionally or financially reliant upon an individual to take care of them. Another form of co-dependency is when a person's satisfaction in life is derived from their ability to please and help other people. This is the type f co-dependency that empaths often suffer from. If you read any books about co-dependency, you will find the characteristics of an unskilled empath described on every page, including:

- Feeling guilt, pity, and anxiety when other people are experiencing problems
- The belief that you are responsible for the choices, well-being, needs, wants, actions, and feelings of others
- Wondering why they don't receive the same treatment from others
- Not knowing how or when to verbalize their wants and needs because they don't know what they are and they don't view them as important as everyone else's
- Doing things for other people that they don't want to do and then getting angry about it
- Feeling compelled to help people whether they ask for it or not and refusing to accept help from others because they feel guilty
- Feeling sad because they pour so much into others, but they don't receive the same back from others
- Feeling empty or useless when they don't have a problem or crisis to resolve or someone to help
- Needy people are always attracted to them
- Putting others' needs before their own
- Feeling used, unappreciated, victimized, and angry

These co-dependent characteristics describe the unskilled empath because empaths have an innate inclination to want to make things better; they are natural healers. But putting so much energy into restoring and pleasing other people is emotionally draining. Empaths need to cut themselves off from this behavior and understand that happiness comes from within and nowhere else.

For example, Mike comes home from work after a bad day, and instead of greeting his wife, he stomps up the stairs, goes into his room, and slams the door. Susan, his wife, is an empath, and she automatically detects that there is something wrong because she starts to feel his pain. She does everything she can think of to make him feel better, but nothing works. Every day, he comes home in the same bad mood. Susan spends her days looking for solutions to a problem she doesn't understand, and her evenings trying to implement them. Her life is centered around her husband and improving his mood. This is what co-dependence is like for an empath. Susan can break her back trying to rectify her husband's problem, but if he is unwilling to talk about it and it is due to a stressful situation at work, until he decides to open up or do something about it himself, there is nothing she can do to help him. The real solution is that Susan must learn to live independently from her husband's problems.

Have you been through a similar experience? Maybe the emotions of others are making it difficult for you to get things done. When you run into situations like this, you need to evaluate the problem to see where it is coming from because, like the example with Mike and Susan, there are going to be times when there is nothing you can do to actively resolve the situation. Your only option will be to offer your support and give your friend or partner the space to deal with their issues. Since you are an energy sponge, you should keep your distance from that person until they have gotten over the crisis. You can still support them without compromising your emotional wellbeing.

DAILY YOGA

Yoga is a powerful method to help get rid of unwanted energy. The combination of postures, deep breathing, and relaxation are essential to releasing tension and blocked energy. To release yourself from holding onto pain, whether it's yours or someone else's, you must let your life force travel freely within your body. So here are a few tips to get you started. You can also buy books, DVDs, or join a yoga class.

Basic breathing technique

- Sit on the ground, cross your legs, straighten your back, and place your hands over your knees.
- Close your eyes and take a deep breath in through your nose—your stomach should rise when you do this.
- Hold your breath for four seconds.
- Breathe out for four seconds—your stomach should deflate when you do this.
- Repeat this for five minutes.

Yoga poses to release negative emotions

Here are three yoga poses to help you release negative energy and allow positive energy to flow freely throughout your body.

1. **Facing Upwards Dog**

   To get rid of unwanted emotions, effective communication is essential. This yoga position helps to relieve tension in the throat and unblock and balance the throat chakra.

   - Lay a mat down on the floor.
   - Lie on your stomach, extend your legs behind you, and push the front of your feet into the ground.

- Position your hands flat on the mat directly underneath your shoulders.
- Inhale and use your hands to push your upper body up off the ground.
- Once you are in an upwards position, exhale.
- Stay like this for 10 seconds at the same time inhaling and exhaling.

2. **Angle Bound Pose**

Much of our emotional energy and trauma is held in our hips. The angle bound pose will loosen up your hips and help move stuck energy throughout the body.

- Sit in a crossed leg position on your mat but allow the soles of your feet to touch.
- Place your hands over your feet and split them apart as if you are opening a book.
- Take a deep breath in and stretch your spine upwards.
- Exhale and relax your knees allowing them to fall towards the ground.
- Repeat this for 10 breaths.

3. **The Plank Pose**

The plank pose helps to strengthen your core, and it is good for the central nervous system. When our bodies feel strong, we also feel strong emotionally and mentally, which allows you to cope with any challenges that may come your way.

- Lie on your stomach with your palms on the floor directly under your shoulders.
- Your legs should be extended behind you (shoulder width apart) with the balls of your toes pressing into the ground.

- Inhale and push your entire body off the ground using your hands and feet.
- Remain in this position for 10 seconds at the same time inhaling and exhaling.

TURN YOUR HOME INTO A PROTECTIVE HAVEN

You should feel safe in your personal space; it is important that you create an environment that you are totally comfortable in. The mood and atmosphere of your home should reflect the way you feel inside. If you are not happy with your living quarters, you are going to have to make some changes.

What does your wardrobe look like? Your drawers? Underneath your bed? Are things just stuffed and piled up all over the place? As you have read, energy travels and attaches itself to objects, people, and other energy. When you are in an environment with a lot of negative people, you start feeling exhausted, hopeless, depleted, and distressed. When you are in an environment with positive people, you feel a sense of calm; you feel healthy and in control of your energy. Now let's take a look at how an untidy and tidy home can make you feel.

A Cluttered and Dirty Home...

Makes you feel exhausted. An untidy home is similar to an energy vampire. Negative energy attaches itself to objects, and simply being in such an environment will drain you.

Makes you feel hopeless. A never-ending pile of mess is psychologically overwhelming. You feel as if you will never get through it all so there is no point in even trying to clean it

A Tidy and Organized Home...

Makes you feel calm. You can relax and unwind in a tidy home. There is space to do things, and you know where everything is. When you walk into a hotel room, you immediately feel a sense of peace because the environment is tidy and organized.

Makes you feel healthy. Dust and mold accumulate in messes. Are you always coughing and sneezing? Do you suffer from allergies? It's probably because you are breathing in all the dirt in your home. Give your home a spring clean and your health issues will improve.

Makes you feel in control. How does it feel when you know where everything is? Clutter prevents positive energy from flowing through your home. Remember, energy attaches itself to objects, and negative energy is attracted to mess, which creates exhaustion, stagnation, and exasperation. What does it feel like when negative energy is stuck in your body? You want to lie in bed and shut the world away because everything becomes more difficult and you can't explain why.

Here is how decluttering your house will unlock blocked streams of positive energy:

You will become more vibrant. Once you create harmony and order in your home, you will feel more radiant and present. Like acupuncture, which removes imbalances and blockages from the body to create more wellness and dynamism, clearing clutter removes imbalances and blockages from your personal space. When you venture through spaces that have been set ablaze with fresh energy, you are captured by inspiration, and the most attractive parts of your personality come to life.

You will get rid of bad habits and introduce good ones. All bad habits have triggers. Do you lie on your bed to watch TV instead of sitting on the couch because you can't be bothered to fold the laundry that has piled up over the past six months? Or because the bed represents sleep, and when you come home from work and get into bed, you are going to fall asleep instead of doing those important tasks on your to-do list. Once you tidy the couch, coming home from work will allow you to sit on it to watch your favorite TV program but get up once it's finished and do what you need to do.

You will improve your problem-solving skills. When your home has been opened up with a clear space, it's easier to focus, which provides you with a fresh perspective on your problems.

You will sleep better. Are you always tired no matter how much sleep you get? That's because negative energy is stuck under your bed amongst all that junk you've stuffed under there. Once you tidy up your bedroom, you will find that positive energy can flow freely around your room making it easier for you to have a deep and restful sleep.

You will have more time. Mess delays you. An untidy house means you are always losing things. You can't find a shoe, a sock, or your keys, so you waste time searching for them, which makes you late for work or social gatherings. When you declutter your home, you could save about an hour a day because you will no longer need to dig through a stack of items to find things.

Your intuition will be stronger. A clear space creates a sense of certainty and clarity. You know where everything is, so you have peace of mind. When you have peace of mind, you can focus on being in the present moment. When you need to make important decisions, you will find it easier to do so.

It might take some time to give your home a deep clean, but you won't be sorry for it once it's done.

CHAPTER 5:

HOW TO BECOME AN ASSERTIVE EMPATH

The word assertive means *"having or showing a confident and forceful personality."* Assertiveness is a powerful quality to have, and even more so if you are an empath. Empaths can be so kind that they neglect themselves. Highly sensitive people understand the negative effect that conflict has on their energy. Just being present when there is a disagreement or an argument can cause them severe distress. Therefore, empaths stay away from any type of conflict even when their beliefs are challenged. This is one of the reasons empaths are targeted by manipulators—they would rather agree with you than get into an argument. This is why assertiveness should be a part of your character. It will ensure that you don't allow others to walk all over you and that you are capable of standing up for yourself when necessary.

STAND UP FOR YOURSELF

The average person doesn't understand empaths; in fact, most people have never heard of the term and have a tendency to label highly sensitive people as mentally challenged. This type of judgment can lead empaths to feel ashamed of their gift, keep quiet about it, and try and act as if it doesn't exist. In reality, a lot of people wish they had the ability to tune into the emotions of others; it would make life a whole lot easier, especially in romantic and work relationships. Imagine being able to detect when your significant other is feeling down, even though they haven't said anything? Or knowing when not to send your manager that email about a pay raise because they are not in the best of moods?

Empaths shouldn't be ashamed of their ability. They should embrace their gift and be proud of it. Don't allow others to look down on you for the sake of avoiding conflict. I am not saying you should get involved in full blown arguments about your abilities, but spend time educating yourself about your gift, so that you feel more confident when explaining it to others. Another aspect of being assertive is that you know who you are, you are confident in your own skin, and you are not going to conform to anyone else's standards but your own.

Repressing your emotions can have a negative effect on your psyche, and this is something that empaths do to avoid conflict. They get into situations where they should have verbalized their disagreement of something but failed to do so in case an argument broke out. One way to get over your fear of defending yourself is to change your definition of conflict. It is natural to disagree with people. We are unique beings with different opinions, ideas, and perspectives, so we are bound to challenge each other every once in a while. Instead of seeing conflict as something negative, look at it as a normal part of life. People stand up for their rights and for what they believe in every day. In fact, you will gain more respect if you speak up for yourself. Even if the other person in the conversation is getting aggressive, you

ond in a calm but assertive manner. No matter how you
ain from showing signs of irritation, anger, or fear, you
don t want to give the impression that what the other person
said has had a negative effect on you.

Let Others Know What You Need

Because empaths are so compassionate and have a tendency to
want to please and help others, people feel comfortable confid-
ing in them. Are you always providing a listening ear to your
friends, associates, and family members when they have a problem? Does this type of interaction leave you feeling emotionally
drained and unable to focus on your daily tasks? Because you
always provide the shoulder to cry on, do you find it difficult to
let those closest to you know when you are hurting?

Letting people know what you need will have a positive
effect on your energy field. You are going to feel uncomfortable
when you first start doing this because it is not something that
you are used to doing. But once you realize how much better it
makes you feel, it will become easier for you. There are going to
be times when your needs inconvenience someone else; there is
nothing wrong with this—let the shoe be on the other foot for
a change. Empaths are always going out of their way to help others, now it's your turn. You should also think about your needs
and how they relate to your health, and constantly allowing people to drain your energy is going to leave you feeling exhausted,
tired, and in the worst case, sick. There is nothing selfish about
thinking like this, as these are steps you are going to have to take
if you want to maintain balance in your life.

Your friends and loved ones should care about your health
needs. Tell them what it's like being an empath because they

probably don't know. Most people are just going to assume that you are an extremely loving and kind person. Let them know your triggers, and the environments and atmospheres you feel uncomfortable in. You should also explain to them how important it is for you to have space. If necessary, block off a day and time during the week and request that no one contact you. When those around you know what you need, they are more likely to respect your wishes.

Empaths often feel uncomfortable letting their friends and family members know when they have a problem because they are always the ones lending a supporting ear. Some empaths even feel guilty when they express negative emotions, which leads you to keep things to yourself and repress your feelings. This is a dangerous way to live because repressed emotions can cause medical conditions such as heart disease and arthritis. You are just as important as anyone else in the world, and you deserve the same time and attention as the next person. A conversation with someone who cares about how you feel will help to recharge your batteries.

You are an extraordinary individual with your own set of aspirations and goals. People are not always going to understand your passions, and the truth is that they don't need to. When it comes to decision making, the people around you are going to have a difficult time understanding your natural intuitive ability to know whether something is right or wrong. This can scare people and cause them to want to make decisions for you in fear that you are making the wrong one. One of the gifts you hold as an empath is the ability to feel when something is wrong or right. Be careful not to allow others to think for you—listen to your inner voice and follow it. When friends and family members attempt to intervene in your decision-making process, let them know in no uncertain terms that your mind is made up and you are not going to change it. Once people start to see that you are capable of making the right decisions, they will begin to respect you and your decisions, and this will increase your confidence.

CHAPTER 6:

HOW TO CONTROL YOUR EMOTIONS

L iving as an empath is like being on a constant emotional roller coaster. One minute you are fine, and the next your head is spinning in a whirlwind of thoughts and feelings, and you are not quite sure where they came from. The good news is that it is possible to control your emotions. You don't need to live in a state of constant turmoil. Here are a few tips to assist you.

DON'T EXPECT EVERYONE TO LIVE UP TO YOUR EXPECTATIONS

As an empath, you've got strong feelings. You can tune in to what people are thinking by reading their reaction, and this can sometimes send your mind into overdrive. Have you ever spent time talking to someone only to find that you can't get the conversation out of your head after you get home? You spend every waking moment going over the details of the discussion and you end up drawing conclusions about how the person feels about you. Nine times out of ten, your brain will trick you into believing that they don't really like you, or that they didn't really agree with what you were saying. You might also feel disappointed that the person you were speaking to didn't feel the same level of compassion as you. But you have to remember that first, you are a highly sensitive person, so things are going to affect you more than they are going to affect others. And second, people are always going to have different opinions—what overwhelms your heart may not overwhelm somebody else's.

We live in a fallen world, nothing is perfect here and it never will be. Ideally, everyone should be kind and loving to one another, but as you know, that's simply not the case. The reality is that there are wicked, narcissistic, and evil people walking the earth who can take a life without thinking twice about it. You only have to turn on the TV or open a newspaper to see how much evil takes place in the world every day. It would be magnificent for you if everyone was an empath, if everyone had the emotional capacity to shoulder the burdens of others, but this is simply not the case. You have no power over the way other people think, and there is no point in wasting your energy trying to change it. When you come to the conclusion that in general people are not going to share the same level of compassion as you, it will make your life a lot easier because you won't spend so much time living in disappointment. You will be able to brush things off and keep moving.

Not everyone is going to agree with you. In fact, some of your friends and family are going to make decisions that are in direct conflict with yours. You will decide to go one way, and they will decide to go another, and there is absolutely nothing wrong with this. When it happens (because it will), let it go. Everyone is entitled to their own opinions and has their own life decisions to make, whether you agree with them or not. You might feel in your spirit that a friend is making the wrong choice, so unless they ask you to intervene, leave them to it. Some people will have to learn the hard way and consequence is the best teacher. When you try to convince others to do something that is against their will, you waste a lot of energy. Situations like this leave you feeling drained and exhausted.

Not forcing your expectations on others is one of the most important life lessons I have learned. There is nothing more time consuming than trying to get others to see things from your point of view. It's a waste of time, parallel to speaking Chinese to a man who only speaks English—they will never understand! And that's ok. When it comes to your expectations, the only person you should be concerned about living up to them is you.

HAVE YOUR TOOL KIT WITH YOU AT ALL TIMES

There are plenty of tools available for empaths to use in everyday situations. To make life easier for yourself, you should have them ready and available to use at all times. If you are sensitive to temperature, light, or sound and you know you have to leave the house, make sure you take what you need with you. If you drive, I would advise that you keep a spare set of these items in the car, so you don't have to worry about packing them every time you leave the house.

If you are sensitive to loud noise, carry noise-canceling headphones. If you don't have a pair already, you can buy small discreet earbuds that you can wear in any environment. Carry a sweater, cardigan, or t-shirt in case the temperature changes. Empaths can find it distressing when they are too hot or too cold.

Preparation is your best defense against protecting your energy. You will experience less anxiety when you know that you have everything you need just in case of an emergency.

SET LIMITS WITH TECHNOLOGY USE

Empaths may love technology more than anyone else. Since they like to isolate themselves, it allows them to communicate without being present in social situations. But it also has its downsides. When you are constantly available online, it gives energy vampires easy access to you, and that is definitely something you want to avoid. Also, people can post the most distressing and heartbreaking news on social media. In recent years, several violent deaths and suicides have been posted online. Sometimes, energy vampires are not people, but the platforms that you are constantly scrolling. Do you ever feel drained after looking through your Instagram or Facebook feed? It is possible for you to absorb negative energy when you spend too much time online.

Setting limits or abstaining from social media for a period of time can promote mental clarity and restore energy levels. Set yourself a technology time limit of 30 minutes to one hour per day. This is just enough time to do what you need to do without getting sucked into all the drama that takes place online.

HOW TO RESTORE YOUR ENERGY

One of the negative effects of being an empath is a constant loss of energy. You can avoid this when you need to. But a natural part of being an empath is opening your energy fields for the greater good, which will leave you feeling drained. The good news is that there are techniques you can incorporate into your life to restore your energy levels. The healing process no longer solely involves medicine and therapy; people seeking help now have a range of options to choose from. Here are a few practical techniques that can assist you in maintaining balance and restoring your energy levels.

Acupuncture: Empaths often suffer from digestive and lower back pain because of the negative energy they carry in these areas. Acupuncture is an ancient Chinese treatment, and one of the many ways in which it works is through balancing vital energy. It involves inserting needles into certain parts of the body to promote the free flow of energy. Acupuncture improves the circulation of oxygen and blood throughout the body, which promotes energy production at the cellular level. Additionally, acupuncture improves the digestive function, which is vital to providing essential nutrients that support energy production to the body.

You may have heard of the term "chi." Ancient Chinese practitioners use it to refer to a person's energy or balance. Acupuncture treatment is deeply relaxing. It brings the body's system back into alignment creating a healthy balance that enables energy levels to recover and rebuild themselves.

Your mantra: Empaths possess the unique ability to read people with precision and accuracy. However, they find it difficult to understand their own emotions. Mantras are short powerful statements that remind you of your life's direction. They are more than inspirational quotes that provoke people to take action. They are powerful words that call what you want into your reality. Some empaths will not engage in social activities or spend time with people unless they have repeated their mantra. Here are some powerful mantras that you might want to consider using:

- I control where my energy goes, and I will not allow others to take it from me.

45

- I have the confidence to express what I need and defend myself when necessary.
- I will disassociate myself from toxic situations without feeling ashamed.

Once you have chosen your mantra(s), get into the habit of saying them every day. You might feel a bit strange saying them at first because, in reality, you don't actually believe the words that are coming out of your mouth. But the more you say them, the more you will start to believe them, and they will eventually become a part of your core belief system.

I love mantras because you have full control over what you say. Spend some time defining your own mantras. You will be surprised at how much fun you have with them.

Palliative care: Palliative care is also known as "supportive care." It is treatment, support, and care for terminally ill patients. The aim is to improve quality of life by being as active and healthy as possible in the time they have left. It can involve:

- Managing painful physical symptoms
- Psychological, spiritual, and emotional support
- Support for family and friends
- Help with things such as eating, dressing, and washing

Ok, so you are probably thinking that being an empath is not a terminal illness, so how is palliative care going to help me? Well, another aspect of palliative care is palliative arts, which involves engaging in purposeful activity to add meaning and enrich life. This type of therapy involves patients dealing with their emotions through activities such as sculpting, painting, writing poetry, and listening to music. This enables them to focus on their negative emotions by expressing them in a positive light. Since empaths are typically creative people, this is a great way to relieve some of the tension associated with being a highly sensitive person. Empaths also find it difficult to express negative emotions to others, so this is another way of releasing energy that does not benefit you without the fear of being judged.

> *Change your thought process:* Your thoughts dictate your actions, so if you want to change the way you react to certain situations, you are going to have to change the way you think. This is easier said than done because our thought patterns stem from years of social conditioning. When people or situations are overstimulating, it is easy to ignore it or justify it by accepting that this is "just the way things are," when in reality, you should have taken some type of action. There are also going to be times when you are so used to helping other people that compassion has become your crutch. For example, a friend of yours is in an abusive relationship. Every other week she is calling you crying about the latest fight she just had with her boyfriend. You keep telling her to get out of the relationship, but she keeps going back. You keep answering the phone even though speaking to her is draining because you feel her pain and want to help her to overcome it. But the reality of the situation is that there is nothing you can practically do to help her; she has to make her own decisions.

By changing the way you think about things, you change your reality. The way you look at situations and your tolerance levels will also change. No longer will you allow people to treat you as a dumping ground for their problems. The bottom line is that your mind is not a trash can, and when people are constantly offloading their issues onto you that's what they are indirectly saying. Remember, garbage in, garbage out. Whatever you allow into your system consistently is what is going to come out. One of the main reasons empaths always feel depleted is because they let too many people dump their rubbish onto them. You will start recognizing your own self-destructive behavioral patterns and adjust them before they start to have a negative effect on your life.

How do I Change the Way I Think?

Changing the way you think is not an easy process—it takes time and practice. In the field of psychology, this is referred to as cognitive behavioral therapy (CBT). The treatment takes a hands-on and practical approach to problem-solving. The end goal is to change the behavior and thinking patterns that contribute to the issues that people are dealing with. It is used to treat a range of psychological illnesses such as anxiety, depression, insomnia, and addiction. CBT works by changing a person's attitudes and behavior by focusing on the thoughts and beliefs that are held by the patient. This is called "cognitive processes," and they are evaluated to discover how a person handles emotional problems.

You don't need to see a therapist to practice cognitive behavioral therapy. You can if you wish, but there are plenty of books that will walk you through the process. In the meantime, here are some steps that you can put into practice immediately.

RECOGNIZE YOUR THOUGHT PATTERNS

Negative thinking leads to stress, fear, anxiety, and a whole host of unwanted emotions. Once you learn to identify the negative thought patterns as they happen, you can step back from them. This process is called "cognitive defusion," where you learn to see the thoughts in your head as thoughts and not reality. The problem is that we don't realize how powerful our thoughts are. We can become so attached to them that they play out in our everyday lives. When we can step outside of ourselves and look at our thoughts for what they really are, and only listen to them if they add value to our lives, things will start to change for the better.

The first thing I want you to know is that there is nothing wrong with having negative thoughts. I know that sounds like an absolute contradiction to everything you have just read but hear me out. If you look back into human history when we were hunters and gatherers, the mind was programmed to look out for dangers and problems. Our ancestors didn't live in houses where they could keep the door locked at night, so they had to protect themselves against wild animals, which meant that they were constantly thinking about new protection strategies. Now, there is nothing positive about thinking a 10-foot bear is going to come and eat you and your children in the middle of the night is there? But, unfortunately, that was their reality. They had to think like that to outsmart the wild animals. Today's problems are much different. We no longer need to worry about predators attacking our families in the middle of the night, but we still need to think about protection strategies. For example, a husband and wife have to think about what would happen if one of them were to get sick or die. This is why people get insurance—to make sure they are covered if the worst does happen. There is nothing positive about anticipating death, but it is a reality everyone has to think about, and if you don't, you will end up stuck in a rut when something does happen.

The problem isn't the thought, the problem is believing that these thoughts are true. So, for example, back to your friend who won't leave her bad relationship. You lie awake at night thinking about it. Your main concern is that if she doesn't leave him, she could get seriously hurt or worst-case scenario, he might kill her. There is nothing wrong with thinking like this because it is normal to worry about your friend. The problem is that you feel that you have to cater to her every need any time she calls. Your thought process is if you don't answer the phone, she won't think you are a good friend, or that she won't be able to cope without you. You are so attached to your thoughts that you believe them wholeheartedly, and so you pick up the phone every time she calls and allow her to dump her trash on you.

The reality is that you don't know what your friend is thinking and neither do you know if she will be able to cope if you don't continue to baby her. So, because you don't know this as a fact, they are simply thoughts that you can allow to pass by without focusing on them. Now that you have come to this conclusion, you are free to lie in bed at night and think about something that edifies you instead.

Most people have become so used to negative thinking that it has become a habit. They don't even know when they are doing it, so you have to train yourself to recognize unhelpful thinking patterns. Here are some of the most common, how to recognize them, and what you can do to stop them from dominating your mind.

NEGATIVE SELF TALK AND CRITICISM

It is often said that we are our own worst enemy—this is a very true statement. You may think that you spend the majority of your time talking to your significant other, but the truth is that the majority of your time is spent speaking to yourself! I thought this was the most ridiculous statement I had ever heard when it was first introduced to me, but the more I analyzed it, the more it made sense. You see, each one of us has an inner voice, and depending on how we tune in, it can be either positive or negative.

Negative self-talk and criticism is when you are constantly berating yourself. You highlight all your flaws and tell yourself that you are not good enough, and neither will you ever be good enough. You beat yourself up because you haven't reached your idea of perfection. Empaths probably suffer from this more than most, especially when they can't fix other people. They feel as if it's their fault and that the reason the other person is failing is because they can't come up with the right solution to their problems. This leads to feelings of low self-worth and low self-esteem.

There is nothing wrong with wanting to help people, but you have to realize that first, you can't help everyone, and second, no matter what you do, some people will only change when they decide to. When the mind is continuously focused on what you are not capable of, you will invite more of these things into your life.

LET GO OF OTHER PEOPLE'S PROBLEMS

For empaths, this line of negative thinking is a lot different. As mentioned, they spend a lot of time and energy trying to resolve other people's issues. You can become so focused on other people that you neglect to take care of yourself. You are always thinking about a friend or a family member's problem and punishing yourself mentally if you can't find a solution. For example, you have everything going for you, a nice home and a nice family, but your friend's car breaks down and she is extremely upset about it because she doesn't have the money to fix it. So now all you can think about is how you can help your friend raise the money to fix her car. You forget how fortunate you are to have what you have, gratitude goes out of the window and you spend your time frustrated and depressed because of a problem that doesn't even belong to you!

STOP BEING A PERFECTIONIST

Have you ever attempted to count the number of stars in the sky? If you haven't, take a shot, you will soon find out that it's impossible! Well, perfectionism is exactly the same; it is impossible to achieve. In fact, it is an unpleasant obsession that messes with your emotions, decision making, interactions, and makes overall mental clarity difficult. It is simply unrealistic to try to be perfect in an imperfect world.

For the majority of individuals, the desire to be perfect is something that was instilled in them from childhood. This might have been a parent who expected their kids to be straight "A" students or a father who put unrealistic expectations on his wife to ensure that the house was kept in immaculate condition. In general, there is nothing positive about these experiences. When the expectations were not met, there was no positive reinforcement but negative feedback, which damaged the child's self-esteem.

This type of child rearing will cause lasting damage to all children, but even more so to those who are highly sensitive. It leads to an intense self-hatred because they are unable to meet the unrealistically high expectations of their parents.

There is nothing wrong with having a desire to do things properly and wanting to be proud of your efforts. Such people are referred to as high achievers; however, many empaths suffer from perfectionism. Here are some of the character traits of a perfectionist:

Unrealistic standards: Being a high achiever is fantastic. Everyone deserves not only to want the best for themselves but to achieve it. The problem is that perfectionists tend to set unrealistic goals for themselves. High achievers set high goals for themselves, and once they have achieved them, they might have some fun and set a goal that's even higher than the last, and enjoy reaching it. Perfectionists' goals are typically so outlandish, it's virtually impossible to meet them so they become unhappy and uptight. This is one of the main reasons high achievers are not only more successful but happier than the perfectionist when it comes to goal attainment.

Procrastination: It makes no sense that a perfectionist would also be prone to procrastination. This is something you don't want to do if you want to achieve your goals. But the strange thing is that procrastination and perfectionism go hand in hand because of the fear of failure. They will spend all their time anticipating what could go wrong and what failure would look like. This leads to immobilization, and nothing ends up getting done, which leads to a feeling of failure and a vicious cycle begins.

Low self-esteem: Perfectionists are very self-critical; the slightest little thing can go wrong, and they will beat themselves up for days. They think they are not worthy of anything good happening to them. Their overall sense of personal value is already low, so when things don't go the way they had planned, they use that as an excuse to validate their feelings of low self-worth.

Push vs. pull: High achievers and perfectionists set goals for different reasons. The desire to achieve a goal pulls high achievers to accomplish theirs. Whereas the fear of not achieving pushes perfectionists towards their goals. In addition, if they do not reach their goals according to the perfect standards they have set for themselves, they view their efforts as a failure.

All or nothing: There is no such thing as "almost perfect" to a perfectionist; anything less than perfect is considered a failure to them. High achievers, on the other hand, work hard towards their goals and are satisfied even if things don't go according to plan. As long as they know they tried their best, a high achiever will always be content.

Defensiveness: Perfectionists can't take constructive criticism; they assume that they are simply being criticized and this hurts them deeply. High achievers, on the other hand, view constructive criticism as valuable information to help them improve in the future.

So, now that you have worked out that you are a perfectionist, you need to get over it because it can make life as an empath very difficult for you. Here are some tips to help you overcome perfectionism:

Get rid of whatever promotes perfectionism in your life. What are the things in your life that encourage you to be a perfectionist? Maybe you watch TV programs or read magazines that make you feel as if you are not good enough? This may not be intentional, as there is some media that contains a lot of subliminal messaging and just seeing a picture of a woman in a bikini can lead you to start subconsciously comparing yourself to an unrealistic ideal. It might even be the books you are reading or the podcasts you are listening to. Take an inventory of everything you watch, listen to and read and evaluate whether any of these media outlets could be harming you.

Evaluate your friendships. Are your friends high achievers or are they perfectionists like you? If you have more friends that exhibit the same traits as you, you may need to stop spending so much time with them. The people you associate with on a regular basis have a huge influence on you. You need to surround yourself with people who are not going to encourage or justify your behavior but with those who are not going to tolerate it and will tell you when you are saying or doing things that will not benefit you.

Become your own ideal. We live in a world with unrealistic expectations. Everywhere you look there is an image of the ideal man, the ideal woman, the ideal relationship…and the list goes on. If you have lived in this world long enough, you will know that there is no such thing as perfection—it just doesn't exist. There is nothing wrong with wanting the best out of life and working hard to make sure that your goals and your dreams are fulfilled. However, there is something wrong with continuously comparing yourself to the world's unrealistic standards. This leads to feeling that you are not good enough and that, no matter how hard you try, you will never be good enough because there is always a new ideal that you have to aspire to. The best way to handle this is to become your own ideal! In other words, become the best version of yourself, and compete with yourself to become better and better. You can do this by learning new skills to get a job promotion or a new job, going to the gym and improving your physique, or changing your wardrobe every few months. Whatever it is you feel you need to do to improve yourself, go ahead and do it. Once you have done this for a while, you can give yourself yearly evaluations:

- Look at how much you have improved in different areas of your life from the beginning of the year until now.
- Look at the things you have overcome.
- Appreciate yourself and keep your focus on your goals instead of on what other people around you are doing.

Realize that you are hurting yourself and others. Perfectionists not only place unrealistic expectations on themselves, they place them on others as well. So, you are not only hurting yourself, but you are hurting other people as well. There is absolutely nothing healthy about expecting other people to meet your standards. By doing so, you are asking them not to be themselves, but to be who you want them to be. If you are frustrated in any of your relationships, whether it's an intimate one, a friendship, or a family relationship then you might need to think about what you are expecting from them.

Understand that you are only human. Empaths have a tendency to forget that they are human. One of the reasons for this is that their gift is basically a superhuman one. The majority of people are not capable of doing what an empath can do, so your gift sets you apart from ordinary people. The thing you have to remember is that most people are reasonably balanced, as in they accept that people have flaws and make mistakes, so they are not going to judge you if something goes wrong. Unfortunately, there are going to be times when you fall short of your best. But instead of beating yourself up about it, learn to accept that it's good enough. If you know that you have put your best efforts forward, be happy with what you have accomplished and keep it moving.

LEARNING TO FORGIVE

Whether it's a simple disagreement with your partner or a long-held grudge against an old friend, unresolved conflict can cause more damage than you realize. Forgiveness is huge when it comes to controlling your emotions—think about it for a minute. If the person who has offended you invokes certain feelings whenever you think about them or see something that reminds you of them, you are going to be on a constant emotional roller coaster. Not only is this bad for your mental well-being, but it is also bad for your physical health. Some people actually think that it makes them feel good to hold bitter feelings towards someone, but scientific studies have proved otherwise.

Karen Swartz, M.D., the director of the Mood Disorder clinic at John Hopkins Hospital claims that remaining in a continuous state of anger puts the body into fight or flight mode. This results in changes in blood pressure, heart rate, and immune response. These changes then increase the risk of diabetes, heart disease, depression, and other conditions. Forgiveness reduces stress levels, which improves health.

Is Forgiveness Possible?

Yes, it certainly is, people have done so successfully in the past and they continue to do so today. There is more to forgiveness than saying you forgive someone. You have to make a conscious decision to release negative feelings towards them, regardless of what the person has done to you. Your decision to forgive is not based on whether the perpetrator is truly sorry, or whether they have suffered enough for what they have done. It is an active process on your part. When you let go of hostility, resentment, and anger, you become emotionally available to experience feelings of compassion, empathy, and even affection for the offending party.

Research has found that some people are naturally forgiving, and such people tend to be more satisfied with their lives and experience less hostility, anger, stress, anxiety, and depression. People who hold grudges are more likely to suffer from post-traumatic stress disorder and severe depression, as well as other health conditions. But this doesn't exempt them from training themselves to become more forgiving. According to a survey conducted by the Fetzer Institute, a non-profit organization, 62 percent of adults state that they want to be able to forgive more freely.

How to Incorporate Forgiveness into Your Daily Life

The act of forgiveness doesn't come naturally to most people. It is a choice that you have to make and stick to. You are choosing to extend empathy and compassion to the person who has hurt you. Here are some strategies that will help you to exercise more forgiveness in your life and improve your physical and emotional health.

Understand forgiveness: Forgiveness is an act of kindness. The person who you have chosen to forgive doesn't deserve it, but it's not about them, it's about you. This is not about excusing the behavior of the offending person or living in denial that the incident happened. Forgiveness is about freeing yourself from any negative emotions that you might have towards the individual.

Practice forgiveness: As stated, forgiveness doesn't come naturally to the majority of people—it is something that you are going to have to practice. Forgiveness is progressive; it takes time to develop. Just as you are not going to wake up tomorrow with a six pack because you did 100 sit-ups the night before, you are not going to wake up tomorrow with a heart bursting with forgiveness because you have read this book. You have to incorporate regular "workouts" into your daily routine to experience the benefits.

You can start by making a commitment to live in peace and harmony, which can be achieved by choosing not to engage in negative conversation about the person who has hurt you. You don't need to give them compliments, but if you can avoid saying bad things about them, it will help forgiveness grow within your heart.

You can also get into the habit of changing the way you view people in general. Start seeing each individual as unique, irreplaceable, and special. You can practice this ideology through a humanist philosophy or through your religious beliefs. Cultivating a mindset of placing a high value on human life will make it difficult for you to discount the person who has harmed you.

You can act in a loving way throughout your day, whether it's giving a compliment to a cashier or helping a person with their groceries. By showing love when you don't have to, you invite more love into your life, which in turn makes it easier for you to be compassionate towards people, even if they have hurt you. Turning the other cheek, so to speak, when someone aggravates you during the day can also help you become more forgiving. So instead of giving the finger to the person who cuts you off in traffic, maybe you could smile at them. Or if your partner says something that you don't like, give them a hug instead of firing back.

Remember and reflect: Think about what you have experienced, how the person hurt you, and how it made you feel. You should also think about how you felt before the incident and how you feel now. In what ways has being angry affected you?

Emotional pain comes in many different forms, including low self-esteem, self-loathing, lack of trust, unhealthy anger, depression, and anxiety. It is important to recognize and understand what you have been subjected to because of another individual so that you can work through it. Forgiveness is essential if you want to heal emotionally. Depending on the extent of the emotional pain you are experiencing, you can either come to this conclusion by yourself, or you can get professional help. However you choose to evaluate your pain, make sure it is done in an environment where you feel safe, secure, and supported.

Empathize with the person: If you were or are in an abusive relationship and your partner was raised in a violent household, there is a chance that they may develop abusive habits.

I am in no way telling you to remain in an abusive relationship—please get out as quickly as possible! But once you come to this conclusion, you will gain some insight into their psychological suffering and start to see them as a wounded person. Once you gain an understanding of the hurt they are carrying that led them to this point, it will be easier for you to forgive them because, despite what they have done to hurt you, they did not deserve the abuse they had to endure either.

Find purpose in your pain: No one deserves to suffer, and no one wants to suffer in life, but it happens. One of the most effective ways to deal with pain is to find meaning within it. This is difficult to do because most people are not going to want to find anything positive about the hurt they have endured. However, if you can change your perspective about it, you will reap the rewards. Has it made you a stronger person? Is it easier to empathize with others because you have experienced the same pain? When you can find meaning in your suffering, it helps you find a sense of purpose so now you can say, "Ok, you may have put me through hell, but now I am a better person because of it."

Finding purpose in your pain doesn't mean that you diminish what has happened to you. Take the time to address how you have been hurt and recognize the injustice of your suffering, but don't get stuck there.

CHAPTER 7:

LEARNING HOW TO SET BOUNDARIES

Empaths find it difficult to set boundaries because they don't like to upset, hurt, or offend anyone. In a sense, they are people pleasers, they feel guilty when they say "no," and often burn themselves out trying to help others. Empaths don't like to experience negative feelings. They feel other people's feelings, so when they are not able to help or meet someone else's needs, they feel the same pain as that person, which is what empaths find difficult to deal with.

You spend a great deal of energy worrying about situations. Even if you have a desire to set boundaries, you quickly back out because of guilty feelings. To the empath, saying no feels like a dagger through the heart because they feel responsible for that person's emotional well-being, and so you spend the majority of your life trying to avoid this.

You have perfected this avoidance technique, but the truth is that you are doing more harm than good. When you don't set boundaries from the onset, you allow other people's negative circumstances into your life, which will ultimately lead to your downfall. Before we get into how to set boundaries, let's take a look at what they actually entail.

WHAT ARE BOUNDARIES?

A boundary is the invisible line that separates two people. Boundaries put distance between your needs, feelings, and responsibilities and the responsibilities of others. The boundaries you set tell people what behavior you find acceptable and unacceptable, and how you will allow them to treat you. People who don't set boundaries are often taken advantage of. They are what I have termed "yes, yes people," your wish is their command, they can never say no.

Another way to look at a boundary is like a fence between two neighbors. Here is an example to give you a better understanding: Jason finds his neighbor irritating. She thought she was doing him a favor by taking his newspaper from his driveway and placing it on his doorstep. It was a nice gesture, and he probably wouldn't have minded so much if she didn't pick his flowers as she made her way. Jason was not at all happy about this, but he didn't want to make a fuss, so he left it alone. This went on for a few months, then her dog would find his way into Jason's garden and would poop on the grass and scare the birds away from his bird feeder. Jason continued to suffer in silence because he didn't want to cause any conflict.

The final straw for Jason came when he returned home from work to find his neighbor's children playing in his yard. They were treading on his flowers, yelling, leaving toys and trash on the ground like they were in their own home. At this point, Jason became extremely angry. Jason had no one to blame but himself. He may have felt that he was being nice by choosing to turn a blind eye to his neighbor's transgressions, but in the process, he was getting angry and irritated causing unnecessary harm to his emotional well-being.

Jason didn't set any boundaries, which made him responsible for the way his neighbor was treating him, even though she didn't think there was anything wrong with her behavior. He let his neighbor take advantage of him. What she did and what she allowed her dog and her kids to do was definitely out of line, anyone could see that. However, to start with, you could put her behavior in the gray area, acceptable to some and not to others. She didn't know that Jason didn't like her picking his flowers because he didn't tell her. The bottom line is that when you don't let people know what is acceptable and what isn't, they will undoubtedly jump to the conclusion that you are fine with their behavior.

It would have made life easier from the beginning if Jason had said, "Hi neighbor, I really do appreciate you bringing my newspaper to the door, but I would prefer to get it myself. Also, I don't really like people picking flowers out of my garden." There is nothing rude or confrontational about this statement; it draws a line in the sand that says, "This is how far you can come, but no further." Once this is made clear, whomever you are dealing with will stay on the other side of the line.

There is no point in having boundaries if they are not enforced. You have to let people know that there will be consequences if they don't respect the boundaries that you have set in place. If they are broken, go ahead and dish out the consequences. Some people have no problems accepting boundaries, whereas others will challenge you to see if you are serious. So, after Jason had set boundaries for his neighbor and she continued to break them, he would have to confront her again, and the consequences would depend on the history and the nature of the relationship.

Jason could build a 20-foot wall around his house, and unless his neighbor was prepared to fly a helicopter into his yard, there would be no way for her to get in. The problem with a 20-foot wall is that it would also keep the people Jason wants to see away, like friends and family. Basically, all boundaries should be flexible. They keep the people you don't want out but still allow the people you do want in.

WHY DO EMPATHS NEED BOUNDARIES?

Like Jason, without boundaries, you are going to have dogs pooping all over your lawn. As an empath, you have probably already experienced this with certain people in your life. You know, the ones who just take advantage at every opportunity.

BOUNDARIES PROTECT YOU

One of the many advantages of being an empath is that you have the ability to feel other people's emotions. So, you know when negative energy is about to invade your space. When you set boundaries, you keep out the energy vampires who are constantly draining you of your time and emotions.

BOUNDARIES SHOW YOU VALUE YOURSELF

"Yes, yes people" are very insecure, whether this is conscious or unconscious behavior, they are constantly seeking validation from others, which is one of the reasons they find it so difficult to say no. Empaths often believe they are responsible for how other people feel because they can pick up on it so easily. The truth is, you are only responsible for how you feel, and when you set emotional boundaries, it shows that you are not willing to allow people to take advantage of you.

Boundaries also keep you from burning yourself out—you can't take part in everything. There are going to be social events, committee meetings, and projects that you are going to have to say no to. Your priorities should come first and not everybody else's.

BOUNDARIES ALLOW YOU TO BE TRUE TO YOURSELF

People who don't set boundaries constantly have people in their space even if they don't want them there. When you don't have time to yourself, you can't be yourself because you are either trying to impress someone or cater to their needs, which is not a good place to be. You need to spend time alone so that you can make your own decisions, process your own feelings, and get your needs met.

WHY DO YOU FIND IT DIFFICULT TO SET BOUNDARIES?

We touched on this slightly earlier, but there are some deep-rooted issues that you may not be aware of that prevent you from setting boundaries in your life.

Low self-esteem: Even though you have all these magnificent powers, empaths are often very insecure. Not only do they have to deal with a weird gift that they feel no one understands, but it also leads them to seek approval from others. Empaths want to feel normal. They don't like feeling like a freak of nature, and acceptance from others gives them that feeling. So, empaths have a tendency to put others before themselves. This might sound like a selfless Gandhi-type altruistic act, but when you are doing it for approval, it becomes a problem.

Fear: Setting boundaries is not normal to empaths, as they are constantly allowing people to overstep the mark because they don't like upsetting people. Not only are they afraid of absorbing the other person's negative energy when they say no, empaths are also afraid of the rejection that may come with turning people down.

You don't know how to set boundaries: Some people simply don't know how to set boundaries. You may have grown up in a household where boundaries were not set, and so it has become the norm for you. The good news is that you can learn how to set boundaries, and I will show you how to in this chapter.

People pleasing: Empaths don't like conflict, and they would rather say yes to something than upset someone by saying no, even if it is going to be of great inconvenience to them.

OVERCOMING THE FEAR OF CREATING BOUNDARIES

YOU NEED BOUNDARIES! Especially if you are going to survive as an effective empath. And you are going to have to get used to setting them. As I'm sure you already know, people are attracted to your energy and want to be around you constantly, so you are going to have to get used to setting boundaries. Here are some tips to help you overcome this fear:

It's a healthy form of self-love. Everyone has needs and that includes you. Sometimes, you just need space to take care of you, and there is nothing wrong with that. Ask yourself this, do you feel guilty about eating more fruits or vegetables? You are probably staring at the page right now thinking, "What a dumb question!" Well, in the same way eating more fruits and vegetables is good for the body, so is setting boundaries good for your emotional health. If you wouldn't feel guilty for eating a healthy diet, why should you feel guilty about setting boundaries?

Get to know yourself. If you don't spend any time alone, you will never truly know who you are. It's practically impossible to set boundaries if you are so consumed with what everyone else needs that you don't know what you need. Spend time tuning into your feelings and thoughts. Take time out throughout the day to ask yourself, "What do I need?" and "How do I feel?" When you have a better understanding of your wants and needs, you will find it easier to set boundaries.

You are not a therapist. And even if you were, the friends who call you every second of the day are not paying for your services. It may be that with all the problems they seem to have, they might actually need some professional help.

Setting boundaries benefits everyone. Setting boundaries doesn't just benefit you, it's also good for everyone around you. When everyone understands where they stand in the relationship, it makes life a whole lot easier. Have you ever just snapped at someone for no apparent reason? Most people are going to answer yes to this question because one of the consequences of not setting boundaries is never saying how you really feel. So even though what people are doing and saying is getting on your nerves, you keep tight-lipped about it because you don't want to offend anyone. We all have a breaking point, and eventually things just get to be too much, and we end up saying or doing something we regret, and its often over something minor. When this happens, people feel as if they have to tiptoe around you in case you snap again. When you set boundaries and learn how to keep people at a distance, you will have more patience and energy. You won't feel so much resentment and you will be less reactive.

Practice. As you know, practice makes perfect. The more you practice setting boundaries, the better you will get at it. So, keep practicing!

How to Set Boundaries

As you have read, one of the main reasons empaths don't set boundaries is because they don't know how to. The good news is that this is something you can learn. Here are some tips to get you started.

Take time out. The first thing you need to do is take some time out to reflect on your relationships. Get a pen and paper and write down exactly how you feel about each person and why you think they are taking up too much space in your life. Work out whether certain behaviors are the rule and not the exception. When you approach the person, you want to make sure you are not jumping to unnecessary conclusions so that you don't end up offending them.

You can't change people. As much as we would like to mold and shape people into who and what we want them to be, this is not possible. We can only change ourselves, so there is no point in getting stressed and upset about the things we have no control over. Some of the people in your life are just not going to get it. Even though you create boundaries, they will continue to push them. I am an advocate of the three strikes and you're out concept. If you have to tell someone three times that they are offending you, and they continue to violate you, cut them out of your life. It might sound a bit harsh, but their behavior is evidence that they have little respect for you. Once they realize that you are serious about your boundaries, it might motivate them to change.

What are the consequences? Before you approach anyone, you will have to decide what the consequences of breaking your boundaries will be. For example, if your partner knows that you expect them to be faithful in the relationship, but they go out and cheat, end the relationship. If you tell a friend that you are not available to talk during a certain time frame, but they call you anyway, don't answer the phone. Do you get the point? When boundaries are broken, you must enforce the consequences.

Use the correct language. When you have finally plucked up the courage to speak to this person, make sure you use the right language. People are sensitive, and the wrong words can sometimes have the opposite effect. Use phrases such as, "I want to talk to you about how I'm feeling," or "We need to work something else out because this isn't convenient for me," or "I want to let you know how I feel about..."

Don't get confrontational. In general, empaths don't like conflict; however, as mentioned above, language and the way you approach the situation is important. Stay away from sending your friend a formal invite to a "Boundaries Talk." Using words such as "We need to talk" is immediately going to put people on the defensive. Alternatively, you can use the language suggested above in the right context. Wait until the offensive behavior shows up again such as calling you at

2 in the morning or having you wait two hours while she gets ready. It is at this point that you can share your feelings and lay out your expectations about what you are willing to accept.

Don't compromise. When it comes to setting boundaries, the worst thing you can do is compromise. There should be no, "Ok, I'll do it this time." When you allow people to break your boundaries once or twice, they will continue to do so. When you say one thing but do another, people start to question your character. Once this happens, it will be very difficult for you to establish boundaries because people won't take you seriously.

CHAPTER 8:

HOW TO BECOME AN EXTROVERTED EMPATH

E mpaths are typically introverts, they have a unique way of interacting with the world. They don't really like to socialize, and they refuse to engage in small talk. An introverted empath is never the center of attention; they are quiet at social events and often leave early instead of socializing with people they don't feel comfortable with. If they do go out, they will drive themselves or find their own way there to avoid having to be dependent on anyone to get home.

In contrast, extroverted empaths are more sociable. They are talkative and don't get overstimulated and exhausted when amongst large groups of people. There is nothing wrong with being an introvert, but in general, extroverts are preferred. Those who are lively and outgoing are more exciting to be around and are often labeled as "the life and soul of the party."

Studies have found that dopamine levels determine whether a person is an introvert or an extrovert. Dopamine is a neurotransmitter responsible for several functions in the body, and one of those functions is mood regulation and has therefore been dubbed as the "feel good hormone." Research shows that introverts don't need as much dopamine as extroverts to feel good, which is why they feel comfortable spending time alone, meditating and reading, and they do not need the external stimulation from large social gatherings and parties. Extroverts get their dopamine fix from lively events and prefer to socialize in this way.

There are many reasons an introverted empath would want to become more of an extrovert.

Extroverts are rewarded. As previously stated, people prefer extroverts, which is made evident in the fact that our current culture grants more economic and social benefits to people who are outgoing and bold. The majority of famous people are extroverts; they are gifted and talented and love to be in the limelight. Even if an introvert has the gift of entertainment, they shy away from it because they don't like being in crowds.

Extroverts are happier. According to personality research, extroverts are happier than introverts, there are several reasons for this. One study found that extroverts find love easier so they are happier. Extroverts laugh a lot, which increases their levels of joy.

Extroverts are more confident. To be the life and soul of a party, you need a certain level of confidence, and extroverts have this. They don't care what anyone thinks about them.

What is an extrovert? The assumption is that an extrovert is an outgoing socialite who enjoys being in the limelight. This is true; however, there is much more to being an extrovert. If you want to become one, you are going to need a better understanding of their character traits.

They enjoy social contact. Extroverts need to be around people because this is when they are at their happiest. Socializing is a way of recharging their batteries, and they feel down and depleted when they are alone.

They enjoy novelty, risk, and adventure. Extroverts live life on the edge, and they get bored easily. They are always looking for the next thrill, making them quick to jump into new experiences and activities.

They enjoy working in groups. Extroverts enjoy working in groups. They feel comfortable when they are surrounded by people.

They like attention. Deep down everyone likes attention, but extroverts like it more than most, and will often go out of their way to get it.

The good news is that you can learn to become more extroverted if you want to. You don't have to be a shy introvert forever. Here are some tips to help you build confidence and transition from being a shy empath to an outgoing and sociable empath.

Get out of your comfort zone. In the field of psychology, stepping outside of your comfort zone is also referred to as "the optimal anxiety zone." The theory behind this concept is that when you are slightly anxious, your productivity levels increase. For example, some people do exceptionally well when they start a new job. Because they are not entirely comfortable, they go above and beyond the call of duty to prove that they can do the job.

It can be difficult to find your zone of optimal anxiety. You will need to monitor yourself constantly to discover at which point your anxiety becomes so overwhelming that it hinders your productivity.

An example of your anxiety hindering your productivity is starting a new job without the necessary qualifications or training to do the job effectively. In this instance, you are going to be extremely anxious because you know that you are not qualified for the job, which will have a negative effect on your productivity.

Push yourself. This is similar to number two but slightly different. Pushing yourself means learning and accomplishing things that you are not otherwise comfortable with, or that you didn't think you would be capable of achieving. You need to get comfortable with being uncomfortable. This will help you to embrace extroverted traits such as enjoying adventure and novelty.

However, it is important that you don't go over the top with this because you don't want to scare yourself and quit. Stepping too far outside of your comfort zone can make you anxious, so take it one step at a time. For example, if you like sitting in and watching a movie by yourself, why not invite a friend around instead? The next time invite two friends, and then you can make a trip to the movies. Can you see the progression here?

Challenge yourself. Make challenging yourself a routine in your life. It will teach you to step outside of your comfort zone and find your optimal anxiety level. As your brain becomes accustomed to trying new things, you will become less uncomfortable and begin to embrace the challenges that you set for yourself.

Be spontaneous. Extroverts love adventure and new experiences, but this is not the case for introverts. Before taking action, introverts prefer to think through and plan out every last detail. Again, start small and build up to become more and more spontaneous. For example, you can ask a co-worker that you never really associate with to go to lunch. Or if you are in a relationship, take your partner on a date without planning what you intend to do. As you practice this, you will soon start to get more comfortable with spontaneity.

Plan your group interactions. One of the reasons introverts don't like being in groups is that they get nervous about what to say and how to act. When you know you are going to a social event, plan your interactions beforehand. For example, think about different topics of conversation. Ask open-ended questions such as, "Tell me about what you do for a living." Or if you know that the person you are talking to lives locally, ask them about fun things to do in the area. People like talking about themselves, and open-ended questions are an invitation to make conversation. If you are feeling brave enough, you can also memorize some jokes to tell.

Find new ways to socialize. To make new friends, you are going to have to find new ways to do so. You don't have to go to bars or nightclubs if that is not your preference. Since I am assuming you have an idea of the type of people you would like as friends, you will need to socialize in places where you will encounter them.

Have a meet and greet. Have a small gathering at your house and ask each friend to invite a friend that you haven't met before. In this way, you will be in a comfortable environment with people that you already know introducing you to new people.

Get online. The internet is a great way to meet new people. There are plenty of social networking sites you can join to do this. Once you feel comfortable enough, you can arrange to meet up with some of your new friends offline.

Join a gym class. Gym classes are a bit more intimate than just going to the gym. The classes are small, which will make it easier for you to meet new people.

CHAPTER 9:

HOW TO BLOCK OTHER PEOPLE'S ENERGY

Empaths are blessed with the ability to absorb other people's energy. This means that they can easily detect how people are feeling. When they walk into a room, they can feel the energy of the environment. This is great when you are absorbing positive energy, but when it is negative, it can be very draining. In a sense, empaths are controlled by other people's emotions. When they are around happy people, they are happy, when they are around sad people, they are sad, and when they are around angry people, they are angry. This rollercoaster of emotions wreaks havoc on your mental stability.

When you speak to negative people, you are left feeling depleted and they are left feeling vibrant and lively because you have absorbed their energy and they have absorbed yours. Being alone allows you to feel balanced because you are dealing with your own feelings and not everyone else's. This is one of the main reasons empaths are so unsociable. Taking on other people's problems can become a burden.

Empaths are prone to addiction because they find it difficult not to absorb other people's energy. But when they are drunk or high, they relinquish their ability to feel, which provides false protection because they are damaging themselves physically. Empaths must protect their divine gift by learning how to balance and ground themselves.

Once you become more stable, you can consciously protect your energy, and you can walk into a crowded room without absorbing negative energy. If you have the gift of healing, this will also enable you to heal more people because you won't take on their sickness.

It is essential that you protect yourself as an empath; if not, life will become very difficult. Your sensitive nature can lead you to destroy important relationships and isolate you from friends and family. You need to get into the habit of grounding and balancing yourself daily so that you don't leave yourself open and vulnerable.

TECHNIQUES TO PROTECT YOURSELF

Journaling: Journaling enables you to release stuck energy and connect with your core. Energy is felt in the form of emotions, so when you write down how you are feeling, there will be a change in the energy field surrounding you.

For example, you can write down how you are feeling, and then write down how you would prefer to feel. This process will help you shift your emotions.

Detach yourself: Nothing has the power to affect you unless you allow it to. Therefore, the best way to protect yourself is to avoid getting into situations that you know will drain your energy. Empaths are constantly trying to help people because they feel their pain and sympathize with them. An energy tunnel is created any time you take on someone else's problems.

It is very endearing that you are sensitive to other people's feelings and you want to help them. However, you are not a superhero and you can't rescue everyone. In fact, some people need to go through what they are going through to teach them some important life lessons.

It will take a while for you to detach yourself from other people's emotions because you don't want to cause any offense. But once you learn to do this, you can protect yourself from unwanted negative energy.

Meditation: Meditation is a way to center and connect with yourself. It helps release negative energy and gives you balance. It is not an easy practice; emptying your mind can be very challenging, but once you get it right, meditation will be of great benefit to you. There are different techniques, including mindfulness, concentration, cultivation of compassion, tai chi, walking, and qigong meditation.

Research has discovered that meditation has several health benefits, including:

- Reduced blood pressure
- Less stress
- Reduced blood cortisol levels
- Deeper relaxation
- Increased feelings of well-being
- Less anxiety
- Improved blood circulation

- Reduced heart rate
- Slower respiratory rate
- Less perspiration

These health benefits are great, but in Buddhist philosophy, meditation frees the mind from circumstances that it can't control, such as strong internal emotions. The enlightened or liberated practitioner is no longer bound to experiences or desires, but instead has a sense of inner harmony and keeps a calm mind.

Meditation for Beginners

1. Lie or sit in a comfortable position, you might even want to buy a meditation cushion or chair.
2. Close your eyes. If you are lying down, use a restorative eye pillow or a cooling eye mask for additional comfort.
3. Breathe naturally without making an effort to control how you are breathing.
4. Pay attention to your breathing and how your body moves when you inhale and exhale. Pay attention to your stomach, rib cage, shoulders, and chest. Focus on your breath without controlling its intensity or pace. If your mind starts to drift, bring your attention back to your breath.
5. Meditate like this for two to three minutes, and then increase the time once you become better at it.

Universal vacuum cleaner. You can use this method anywhere at any time. You can even do it when you are having a conversation with someone.

1. Close your eyes.
2. Focus on your energy field to locate stuck energy.

3. Think about a large universal vacuum cleaner sucking the negative energy out of your aura.
4. Fill the empty holes by imagining white light entering your body.

Return to sender: Because empaths absorb other people's energy, the majority of your thoughts and emotions don't belong to you. You don't need to know who it came from to send it back. Simply command it to go to the center of the earth and ask your energy to transform it into light.

Spend time alone: One of the main reasons empaths like spending time alone is to avoid negative energy, but this shouldn't be your only reason. Alone time is a way to re-center and balance yourself and let go of everything that doesn't belong to you.

Spend your alone time filling yourself up with positive energy by reading inspirational books, listening to motivational speakers, meditating, or any other activity that you find rejuvenates and refreshes you.

CHAPTER 10:

HOW TO COPE WITH A FLOOD OF EMOTIONS AT ONE TIME

Have you ever experienced being in a crowded place and it feels like you know what everyone in the room is thinking and feeling? It is so intense that you feel like you are no longer in your own body? Unless you learn how to feel balanced at all times, being an empath can feel like a curse instead of the blessing that it really is. Here are some tips to help you deal with feeling so many emotions at one time.

Take care of yourself: This might sound cliché, but you will be shocked at the number of empaths who don't take care of themselves and then complain that they can't handle the influx of emotions they have to deal with. Your mind, body, and spirit are connected, and they should all be in alignment with one another.

Eating junk food is going to make you feel sluggish, lazy, and irritable. The better you eat, the more powerful your physical body will become. You will have a clear mind and it will be easier to listen to your inner voice. It is also important to exercise. Moving the body helps to release blockage and build-up from the negative energy you have absorbed from other people.

Everyone is different, and you will need to find what suits you best. Eat organic food because it doesn't contain any pre-servatives. I am in no way saying that you should become a veg-an overnight, but consume more plant-based foods than animal products, eat less sugar and processed foods. If you are going to eat meat, make sure it is grass fed, and limit your intake of dairy products (You can read more about this in chapter 14).

Balance and moderation are key. You should never feel as if you are depriving yourself, and you shouldn't become so ob-sessed with it that you become stressed and anxious. Taking care of yourself should be fun and enjoyable, and it will become even more so when you start seeing results.

Visualization and aura cleansing: I don't have enough space to go into detail about this, but what I can tell you is that it works. To get a better understanding and some guided in-structions, go to YouTube and type in "Empath Meditation" and "Aura Cleansing Meditation." There are some really good videos to get you started with this, but here are some basic steps to cleanse your aura.

- Set a timer for five minutes and find a comfortable place to sit down and relax.
- Imagine that a cleansing white light is beaming all over you.
- Imagine that the light is healing you and getting rid of anything that is not benefiting you.
- Make a conscious decision to release anything that doesn't belong to you such as emotions, feelings, thoughts, and experiences.

Cleanse your life: What makes you miserable? Is it something that you can stop doing? What leaves you empty and exhausted? Who makes you feel like this? As you become aware of your abilities as an empath, you will notice that you attract people who drain you emotionally—they are called "energy vampires." Where are you going on a regular basis that drains you, where people are constantly taking from you, but you are not getting anything back? Identify these people and places and eradicate them from your life.

Eliminate things that don't agree with your spirit: Anything that doesn't benefit you, things that you are doing just to please others, has to go. If you are invited to an event or a friend asks you to do something that your spirit doesn't agree with, say no! You are going to feel bad when you turn down invitations because you don't like disappointing people, but the truth is that if your spirit is automatically telling you no, it means that something isn't quite right, and you probably won't enjoy yourself anyway. Think back to how many times you have ignored your instincts, and you arrived at your destination, got bombarded with negative energy, and got home feeling mentally exhausted? You have probably experienced this more times than you care to admit. By getting rid of the things in your life that don't agree with your spirit, you are protecting yourself from having to deal with a multitude of negative emotions that you would rather not experience.

Protection Meditation – The Jaguar Method

There are certain powers you can call upon to give you extra protection when you are in need. Empaths often use this method when they are overwhelmed with negative energy. First, let's talk about why the jaguar is so important.

Who is the Jaguar?

A jaguar is a wild cat species native to North America. It is the third largest cat in the world and the largest cat in the Americas. It is a very powerful animal and kills its prey with one deadly bite to the skull. Like empaths, they prefer to spend time alone, and they only socialize with females for mating purposes.

Jaguar Symbolism

The jaguar is viewed as a symbol of strength and life, as well as several other meanings:

- Rejuvenation
- Beauty
- Loyalty
- Courage
- Spiritual power
- Valor
- Fertility

The Black Jaguar Spirit

The black jaguar spirit is beautiful and graceful; the animal is relentless and fast when it comes to pursuing something that it wants. These are the same qualities the jaguar wants you to have when it comes to fulfilling your dreams and desires in life.

It is also a symbol of the power of silence. It hunts and stalks its prey silently and then pounces when it is least expecting it to.

Therefore, as an empath, it is important to know when to make your presence known and when to stay in the background. The jaguar also represents your strong ability to tune into the vibrations present in the atmosphere. When you are interacting with people, the spirit expects you to be in control of your emotions as well as hear the unspoken words of those you are communicating with. The black jaguar is also a symbol of the secret gifts you should be sharing with the world, which includes your knowledge, strength, grace, power, and beauty.

It is also a symbol of your speed and agility in terms of how you handle certain issues in life. It has a strong ability to understand chaos and help you move through the trials and tribulations that you go through in life.

The black jaguar can stare without blinking, he has big mysterious eyes that can see right through to your soul and discern your innermost thoughts and feelings. It symbolizes how you can reclaim your true power and it teaches you how to trust your instincts.

How to Call Upon the Black Jaguar Spirit With Meditation

When you are in a situation that requires additional protection, I recommend calling on the power of the jaguar for assistance. Use it when you are being bombarded with negativity and feel as if things are getting out of control.

- Get into a calm meditative state by taking long and slow deep breaths.
- Feel the presence of the jaguar as it enters into your space.
- Imagine this powerful, beautiful creature slowly walking around your energy field and creating a barrier so that nothing negative can get in.

- Visualize what the jaguar looks like—its deep black fur, piercing golden eyes, statuesque body, and the elegant intentional way in which it moves.
- Feel secure as the jaguar encircles you.
- Thank the jaguar and know that you can call upon him whenever he is required.

CHAPTER 11:

HOW TO FIND PEACE LIVING IN A CRUEL WORLD

There is no denying the fact that we live in a vicious and evil world. You just need to turn on the television, flip through your local newspaper, or turn on the radio to hear the atrocities that are continuously taking place around us. We are constantly bombarded with images of war, murder, and hatred, and it can become extremely depressing if you focus on it. I can't tell you why the owners of the media are so hell-bent on barraging us with negative content, but I can tell you that there are also plenty of good things happening in the world.

12-Year-Old Boy Feeds Thousands of Homeless People

Massachusetts is a better place because of a 12-year-old boy named Liam Hannon, the pioneer of "Liam's Lunches of Love." In his free time, he travels around the city of Cambridge providing lunch for the homeless. He has given out more than 2,000 lunches in bags that he writes handwritten messages of encouragement on. Liam believes that he is spreading a message of joy and hope to the less fortunate, and he hopes that it will ignite something in them to achieve a better life.

Liam's father, Scott raised $44,000 through a GoFundMe page to buy a food truck so that Liam can expand his operation and travel across Boston to give out free lunches.

450 STUDENTS SERENADE DYING TEACHER

After being diagnosed with cancer, more than 450 students from the Christ Presbyterian Academy in Nashville gathered outside his home to sing Christian songs of worship. Despite his radiation and chemotherapy, Ben Ellis continued to teach his students Latin and Bible studies. This beautiful act of kindness went viral receiving 31 million views after it was posted online.

BROOKLYN BROWN'S BENEFIT PROJECT

Brooklyn Brown is a kindergartner who, as an infant, was diagnosed with juvenile rheumatoid arthritis. When she has an arthritis flare, she finds it difficult to walk, needs help going to the bathroom, and sometimes needs a wheelchair to get around. But despite her illness, Brooklyn has a big heart and puts others before herself. Knowing what it's like to spend weeks in the hospital, she decided to do something to help sick children stuck in hospital beds.

Brooklyn started raising money to buy crayons for the kids so they would have something to do when they were waiting for doctors, nurses, or visits from their family and friends.

YOU BECOME THE CHANGE YOU WANT TO SEE

It is a fact that the world we live in is a very evil place; unfortunately, there is nothing you can do about this. You can't control how other people choose to behave, but you can control your actions. Instead of getting depressed about the wickedness that is so prevalent today, you become the change that you want to see. Choose to radiate love every day, whether it is to friends, family, or strangers, make the decision to do something nice for someone. It doesn't have to be anything major. You could buy a homeless person lunch, buy your mom a bunch of flowers, or help an old lady across the road. The idea is to take positive action and become the best person you can be despite the fact that the world is going crazy.

BECOME A VOLUNTEER

Becoming a volunteer is a great way to show kindness and give back to your community. Volunteering is perfect for empaths because they are such selfless people. Volunteering helps switch your focus and enables you to do what comes naturally to you and put others before yourself. It creates social cohesion bringing communities together, connects people, and unites people of different religions, cultures, and walks of life. If you are an empath who tends to isolate yourself, volunteering is also a way to get you to socialize more.

CHAPTER 12:

MAKING CAREER DECISIONS AS AN EMPATH

The majority of jobs involve working with people, whether directly or indirectly, so you are going to have some human contact. Therefore, empaths often find it difficult to work or find a job that is suitable for them. If you are going to excel, you will need to find work that you enjoy and that, to a certain degree, understands your sensitivities. You need to express your creativity, quietness, thoughtfulness, and intuition instead of trying to fit in and become a part of the crowd, which is what happens in most work environments.

CAREERS THAT EMPATHS THRIVE IN

In general, empaths excel when working alone, in low-stress jobs, or when working for smaller companies. They are also more comfortable working a full or part-time job from home, away from the chaos of an office environment, where they are not micromanaged nor forced to deal with frustrating office politics. They prefer to communicate over the phone, through email or text message to limit face to face interactions. Working like this enables you to plan your own schedule, set your own rules, and take breaks at will when you need to recharge your batteries.

Empaths prefer to be self-employed to avoid being overwhelmed by coworkers, managers, frequent meetings, and demanding schedules. If being self-employed is too risky for you, some businesses allow you to work from home. With advanced technology such as Skype, emails, text messages, and access to the internet, it is not always necessary to work in an office. So, you may be able to split your time during the week so that you are working from home for a few days. One important point to take into consideration is that you need to be careful not to become too isolated when working from home. Neither do you want to overwork yourself, because this is easy to do when you don't have a nine to five schedule. You should also take some time out to socialize with friends and colleagues.

If you are self-employed, you prefer working as artists, health care assistants, editors, writers, and other creative professions. Several musicians and actors, such as Jim Carey, Scarlett Johnson, Alanis Morrissette, and Clare Danes have admitted to being "highly sensitive." Other jobs you might want to consider include plumber, electrician, accountant, virtual assistant, graphic designer, website designer, real estate agent, and business consultant. These professions are fine as long as you are self-employed and can set your own schedule and establish solid boundaries with your clients. Forest ranger work, gardening, landscape design, or other employment opportunities where you are required to make contact with the environment are also good for empaths. You might also want to consider jobs that are focused on preserving the earth and her ecosystems.

Empaths also enjoy work where they help others because of their innate desire to serve people. They find great satisfaction in this type of work as long as they don't absorb the stress of their patients and are able to take time out to nurture their own needs. Empaths often become life coaches, hospice workers, clergy, massage therapists, Chinese medical practitioners, yoga instructors, teachers, social workers, psychotherapists, physical therapists, dentists, physicians, employees of non-profit organizations or volunteers, as well as a host of other jobs that involve caring for people. Empaths are also animal lovers and find it satisfying to work with animals as dog groomers, veterinarians, or in animal rescue.

To really do well in any of the mentioned helping professions, empaths can't afford to take on the symptoms and stress of their patients. They can do this by taking regular breaks to meditate and focus on themselves. You also need to set clear boundaries and limits with your clients and take enough time outside of work to refuel and relax. On the other hand, empaths are likely to find jobs such as firefighters, doctors, nurses, and police officers too stressful. Despite the fact that they involve helping people, there is too much sensory stimulation and continuous physical and emotional turmoil for empaths to deal with.

Empaths are valuable in any profession; however, you must find a career that supports your gifts, skills, and temperament. So, when you are searching for a job, use your intuition to discern whether you are a good fit for the values of the company, the energy, the people, and their overall goals. A job might have all the right credentials on paper, but it has to sit well with your spirit.

CAREERS THAT EMPATHS SHOULD AVOID

A job that you are not suited for will drain your energy leaving you feeling weak, tired, and regretting that you are an empath.

This is something that you want to avoid—you want to protect your gift, not deplete it.

One of the worst jobs for an empath is sales, which is especially true if you are an introvert. Spending too much time speaking to people and dealing with angry customers is too stressful for an empath. Also, empaths absorb people's stress and emotions, which can make them sick. One empath I know said that working as a cashier nearly gave him a panic attack—the crowds, the noise, the bright lights, and the loudspeakers were all too much for him. He had to leave in the first hour of starting his job. Whether it's advertising, selling jewelry or cars, empaths don't enjoy having to be on call all day.

Other careers for empaths to avoid include trial attorneys, executives with large teams to manage, politics, and public relations. As mentioned, empaths are typically introspective, sensitive, thoughtful, and soft-spoken. These high-stress professions value extroverts, aggressiveness, and the ability to engage in small talk.

The mainstream corporate world is also a problem for empaths because such environments have a certain code of honor. Money is their main motivation. They don't value people, and it's a dog eat dog world where individuals will do anything to get to the top. Empaths are independent thinkers and will challenge the status quo if it doesn't feel right to them. They like to understand the reasons behind why a decision has been made so that it feels right to them.

How to Handle Taking Disciplinary Action in a Leadership Role

Being an empath has its positives and negatives when it comes to being in a leadership or management role. You can tap into your employees' emotions and know when something is bothering them, which makes you very relatable. On the other hand, empaths don't like conflict and would rather avoid it if possible, which means that as a manager, there is the potential for your employees to walk all over you, which doesn't look good in the work environment. Unfortunately, there are some things that are inevitable as a leader, and one of them is taking disciplinary action against your employees. Here are some tips to do so successfully.

The best way to ensure that things go the way they are supposed to is to prepare yourself beforehand.

Review the details. This should be your first step. What is the reason for taking disciplinary action against this employee? Has there been a complaint lodged against this person? Are they not being productive on the job? Make sure you have your facts straight before you sit down and speak with the employee. If you need evidence, collect it before the meeting.

Know the HR policies and procedures. Knowing the company policies about the alleged infraction will give you the confidence you need to approach the situation in a professional manner. It means that the employee won't be able to talk their way out of the situation because you have the facts and the company's policies on hand.

Know your objective. There is no point in having a discussion with an employee if nothing is going to come out of it. Even if you are just issuing a formal warning, let the employee know that this is what you are doing, and make sure that it is logged in their file.

Be firm, empathetic but professional. Being empathetic is something that comes naturally to you, so you won't find it difficult to think about what it will be like to take their place. Even if they were at fault, the employee is still going to be nervous, upset, and scared during the disciplinary hearing. Keep this in mind while speaking to them, but also remain firm and professional so they know that the matter is serious.

Once your objective has been achieved, end the conversation. There is no need to let the meeting drag on. Have the meeting, say what needs to be said, and shut it down. As an empath, you are going to feel upset for two reasons—it is in your nature not to want to upset anyone and you are going to feel the person's pain and want to make it right. Therefore, resist the temptation to apologize because it's not your problem. Remember, whatever rules were broken, that employee chose to break them. They have made their bed, now they have to lie in it.

Please bear in mind that if you are currently in one of the professions that empaths should avoid, I am in no way telling you to pack up and leave. That would be totally irresponsible of me. But you can find solutions to make your time at work suit your needs better. When empaths are happy, they become extremely valuable in their chosen field.

CHAPTER 13:

HOW TO DISCONNECT FROM WHAT'S GOING ON AROUND YOU

Although the majority of empaths are introverts and would rather spend their time alone than with groups of people, they are constantly a part of the mix. Not because they want to be, but because it is in their nature. Whether an empath goes to the store, a social event or they are in a lecture hall, they connect to the energy in the atmosphere, and when that energy is bad, it can have a terrible effect on them. Here are some tips on how to disconnect from what's going on around you.

REGULAR CENTERING

The most effective way to disconnect from what's going on around you is through centering. As you have read, when you are triggered into an empathetic state, your energy fields are opened, which causes you to absorb other people's energy and for you to release energy to others.

Centering allows you to take your energy back by closing those openings. It is what Eckhart Tolle refers to as "being present," using mindfulness and focus to bring yourself back into a healthy state. This is where you are completely aware of how you are feeling at that moment in time, and you are focused on yourself instead of what's going on around you. When you are centered, you are less likely to become distracted and get overwhelmed by other people's energy.

How to Center Yourself

The main intention of any energy management exercise is to focus on your intention. It is the power of your intention that centers you. Were you aware that you can control your chakras through the process of visualization? In other words, your thoughts and intentions control your energy field. You make the rules and your energy responds.

Most of us do this without realizing it. Negative thinking depletes your energy, and anything you do that doesn't line up with your morals and values depletes your energy. On the other hand, when you repeat positive affirmations, comfort or empower others, your energy field expands. Your energy reacts to everything you say or do.

This is something you may know in theory, but if you are not practicing it, it won't do you any good. Controlling your energy is not an easy task. If it was, negative energy would have been eliminated from the planet a long time ago.

Regular centering helps you to maintain control of your thoughts and energy. Most importantly it is a constant reminder of what it feels like to be centered. You can then tap into this feeling at will when you get too emotionally attached to what's going on around you. The following steps will help you get centered.

1. *Get quiet:* Still your mind by focusing on your breath for 2 minutes.

2. *Ground yourself:* You can ground yourself through the process of visualization. Imagine the energy of your root chakra whizzing through the earth and wrapping itself around the earth's core, then coming back to you in the same way.

3. *Energy retrieval:* This is where you tell your energy to return to you. Thought energy can be absorbed by past events, fears, loved ones, and people around you. Wait for a few minutes and then call that thought energy back to you.

4. *Close your openings:* You are going to have some openings in your energy field at this point, so you will need to close them. You can do this by imagining white light burning at the heart chakra and then reaching out to close the openings. You might hear doors closing at this point.

5. *Experience your energy:* Focus on being silent within, self-aware, and present. Remain in this state for as long as you can.

6. *Remind yourself that you can do this:* Remind yourself that you can enter into this state any time you feel that your chakras are open and you are absorbing too much energy.

If you feel as if you are carrying other people's baggage, you can release this energy before you center yourself. Follow these steps to do so.

1. Shut your eyes.

2. Say out loud, "God" or "Archangel Michael."

3. Then say, "I now call on the source of power to eliminate any energy that is not mine. It is done, it is done, it is done."

Centering is something that you are going to have to practice, and the more you practice, the better you will become at it. Not only will it enhance your empathetic abilities, but you will also have more control over the energy you are absorbing, and where your energy goes.

To master the art of centering yourself the moment you need to, you will have to be very self-aware and have a deep understanding of your empathy triggers. If you don't have a high level of self-awareness, don't worry, you will learn how to raise it in the next section.

How to Raise Your Self Awareness

Most empaths know that they are empaths, but they don't understand that there is a process to it. This is one of the main reasons empaths don't know how to disconnect. They assume it's natural to be in an empathetic state all the time.

In case you have forgotten, let's go over what happens when you tap into other people's energy.

1. Your empathy is set off by something.

2. The doors to your energy fields are opened up and you start experiencing the energy of another person or persons. This is good if you are trying to help someone because you are better able to empathize with them.

3. The doors to your energy fields should close once your job is done, and you should return to your normal self. If you are an unskilled empath and don't know how to close the doors to your energy field, they will stay open and you won't know that they are open.

So, to turn your empathy off, you must be aware of what is taking place when it is happening. This means that your self-awareness needs to be very precise. You will need to practice this regularly to become an expert at it.

To begin, you need to learn what sets off your empathy. It could be one of the following, or something completely different. When you think about it, you will know what they are.

- Violence or aggression on TV
- People suffering
- Someone who disagrees with you
- Someone who needs you for something

Who triggers your empathy the most? Is it family members and loved ones, or just people in general?

The next step is to pay attention to the empathy process. Observe what happens when you are in an empathetic state. What is your main focus at that particular moment in time and when does it happen? It could be when you are walking down the street, having a conversation with someone in a social setting, listening to a friend's problems, or observing the people around you. It is the norm for empaths to focus on other people, so there is a chance that you may not have noticed how much you do this.

When you realize that you are getting sucked into the vortex of another person's energy, it is at this point that you need to call your energy back. You can do this by pinching yourself and paying attention to the physical sensation, or you can pay attention to a color that you like, a piece of artwork, or a piece of furniture. The more you practice this, the better you will become at it, and it will develop into a habit that helps you subdue your empathy.

You can also call your energy back to you and command the doors to your energy fields to close at that exact moment. Take a minute to observe how you feel and what's going on in your spirit. Visualize the open doors to your energy fields slamming shut. If you can get deep into your visualization, you can also imagine the sound of the doors closing. If not, make an affirmation that it is taking place.

TRANSITIONING FROM THE CONSCIOUS TO THE UNCONSCIOUS

If you have spent time practicing the centering process and you are not getting good results, there is something blocking it from working, and you will need to find out what that is. There will be times when you are unable to turn off your empathy because a part of you wants to keep it on.

You may even experience feelings of guilt when you turn it off. Some empaths feel as if they need to remain in a constant empathetic state because without it, they won't be able to help people the way they need to. If this is how you feel, here are some steps to overcome this fear.

Your gift is a sacrifice. There is nothing fun about absorbing other people's negative energy. In some instances, this is required. If you are constantly taking the world on your shoulders, it will eventually damage you and you won't be any good to anyone.

Empathy should be switched off. Simply put, it is unhealthy to remain in a constant state of empathy. How will you ever get to know yourself if you are continuously submerged in other people's energy? You need alone time.

Minimize co-dependency. Empaths are often co-dependent because they can become so attached to someone else's pain that they almost feel as if it's their pain. You will do everything in your power to help the person out of their situation, not only because you don't want them to suffer, but because you don't want to feel their pain anymore. When boundaries are merged like this, the situation can become very tricky, which is especially true if the other person is also an empath.

CHAPTER 14:

HOW DIET PLAYS A ROLE IN ENERGY

E mpaths who understand the importance of diet consume a vegetarian or plant-based diet, and this is not purely for ethical reasons. When your digestive system is at peak performance, it uses a lot of energy. Meat, in particular red meat, is very difficult to digest. According to the Mayo Clinic, meat and fish can take as long as two full days to fully digest. This is because the fats and proteins they contain are sophisticated molecules that the body finds difficult to break down. By contrast, foods that are high in fiber such as fruits and vegetables take less than 24 hours to digest. They move through the system easily because their natural substances help the digestive system to operate more effectively. This means that after you take your last bite of Popeye's chicken, the body spends much of your precious energy trying to digest it.

Empaths need all the energy they can get since they are constantly being depleted of it. Consuming foods that are full of nutrients and easier to digest is a simple way to give yourself that much needed additional energy boost.

I am not going to tell you what you should and should not eat. I have simply given you the information, and it's up to you what you choose to do with it. Some foods are going to agree with you and others won't, so your first step should be to determine which foods work for you and which foods don't. Most nutrition experts recommend an elimination diet, which is where you cut out certain foods one at a time to zero in on specific sensitivities. Once you have pinpointed the foods that harm, it's time to start eating the foods that heal.

I am not a dietician or an expert on foods, but once I realized that my diet played an important role in my empath capabilities, I began to research and experiment with food. I have found that the following foods work best for me.

- Fruits, especially lemons, limes, tomatoes, avocadoes, apples, mangoes, berries, and bananas
- Raw vegetables, especially celery, zucchini, and red pepper
- Cooked vegetables, especially cauliflower, brussels sprouts, broccoli, string beans, and kale
- Raw greens, especially parsley, basil, lettuce, and spinach
- Garlic smoked tofu
- Grains, especially oatmeal, gluten-free pasta, quinoa, and white rice
- Seeds and nuts, especially raw cashews, almonds, tahini, natural peanut butter, chia seeds, and ground flax seeds
- Organic sauerkraut
- Organic dark chocolate
- Vegan protein powder
- Vegan cheese

- Condiments such as hot sauce, Dijon mustard, and apple cider vinegar
- Olive oil and coconut oil
- Foods rich in vitamin B12 such as nutritional yeast and almond milk

I find the following foods problematic, so I have eliminated them from my diet.

- Red and white meat and fish
- All dairy products including eggs, yogurt, cheese, milk, and butter
- Refined sugar
- Gluten
- Caffeine
- Alcohol

As you will notice from my food list, my current diet leans more in the direction of vegetarian and plant-based. Changing my diet has resulted in better digestion, consistent blood sugar levels, high energy levels (I no longer feel the need to take a nap in the middle of the day), clear skin, reduced PMS, and improved moods. I am also more mentally focused, with an improved ability to concentrate on tasks for longer periods of time.

CHAPTER 15:

TIPS FOR RAISING AN EMPATH CHILD

Empath children are special and unique, but to a parent who doesn't understand the gift, it doesn't come across that way. You may think your child is needy, emotional, and oversensitive. You may have even punished your son or daughter because they tend to act out in ways you don't understand. You want them to be happy but don't think that encouraging their sensitivities will help them in the long run. You may have accused your child of being too emotional (this is especially true for boys) and told them that they will need to grow a thicker skin if they are going to make it in this world.

You have been to counseling, therapy, spoken to friends and family, but you just can't seem to figure it out. The thing is that you love your child and you refuse to give up on them, so you continue seeking answers and fate has led you to this book. This chapter will help you if you are not sure whether your child is an empath, or if you know your child is an empath and want some advice on how to raise them successfully.

SIGNS THAT YOUR CHILD IS AN EMPATH

Always feeling unwell: Does your child always have an upset stomach, a headache, or a sore throat? Are they constantly complaining that they are in pain? Do you walk into grocery stores and your child is fine, then five minutes later they are complaining that something is wrong? Most parents chalk this behavior up to attention seeking, and some doctors have even labeled children as hypochondriacs. However, the reality is that highly sensitive people pick up on other people's illnesses, and they can become so in tune with the other person that they actually start feeling their pain.

Although it can get quite frustrating having a child who is always sick, you should never take it out on them. Now that you know that they are not attention seeking, showing your child that you are concerned, you care, and are there to support them is the most effective way to handle this trait.

Extremely sensitive to the emotions in their environment: Empath children will tap into every emotion that is around them. If you and your husband have had an argument and you are trying to hide your anger from the kids, your empath child will pick up on it. Emotionally, there is nothing you can hide from them. Empath children latch onto things such as energy, atmosphere, and body language.

There is no point in trying to hide your emotions from an empath child because they will pick up on them immediately. What you can do is be as open and honest with them as you possibly can. Obviously, there are some things that children don't need to know. In these circumstances, let them know that there is a problem, and you are trying to resolve it, but try not to avoid telling them because they are too young to understand. With everything else, you will make things easier for you and your child if you tell them the truth.

Very responsible: While you might think that your child just enjoys being helpful, it runs a lot deeper than that. Empaths feel as if other people's happiness is their responsibility, so much so that they will abandon their own needs to go above and beyond the call of duty to help someone. If they can't, they get very upset with themselves. An empath child might take on worries and responsibilities that they are too young to handle. You may have already experienced this, but don't be surprised if you are ever struggling with the bills and your child gets upset because they are too young to go out and get a job to help.

Let your child know that you are grateful for their help but that they are too young to intervene in adult affairs and mommy and daddy have it all under control. Encourage your child to relax and have fun and continue to reinforce that it is not their responsibility to make other people happy. Once you can get your son or daughter to understand this, it will free them to enjoy their childhood without having the burden of feeling they are responsible for other people's problems.

Difficulty sleeping: Are there times when your child finds it difficult to sleep at night? Empath children can become exhausted and anxious if they are overstimulated, including having too many things to do throughout the day without taking enough breaks, multi-tasking, and no alone time. They then find it difficult to wind down at night because they are still feeling the stimulation in their system from earlier in the day.

Empath parents are not the only people who struggle to get their kids into bed on time—it is a common problem. The only difference is that empath children are not being defiant when they don't want to go to bed, they simply find it difficult to go to sleep. Here are some tips to help you with this.

Establish a Night Time Routine. Children need structure; it provides them with a sense of security and safety when they know what's coming next. A bedtime routine will help your child develop sleep associations to let them know that it's time to go to bed. A good routine might include:

- Taking a bath
- Brushing their teeth
- Putting on pajamas
- Getting into bed
- Reading a story
- Goodnight hugs and kisses

You can change the routine depending on what works best for your child. It's important to remember that it's not what you do during the routine, but how consistent you are with it.

Avoid stimulating drinks. One of the main ingredients in soda is caffeine, and if you allow your child to drink a can of soda, make sure you give it to them early on in the day so that it doesn't affect their ability to sleep.

Turn off electronics. Kids love gadgets just as much and if not more so than adults. If allowed to, they will continue to play with them right up until bedtime. The light emitted from the screen emulates daylight and tricks the brain into thinking that you should be awake. All electronic devices such as games, laptops, and televisions should be switched off and locked or removed from the room an hour before bedtime.

Provide a good sleeping environment. Your child's room should be conducive to sleep. Ideally, the room should be cool, dark, and quiet. Some children don't like sleeping in the dark, so in such cases, a small lamp would be appropriate. Soft playing nighttime music will also help your child fall asleep as well as drown out any of the other sounds in the house.

They find it difficult to tolerate noise: Are you getting frustrated because your son doesn't like going to the game with you? This isn't because he doesn't like sports, but because he is unable to tolerate crowds, clapping, cheering, booing, and loud music. Basically, noise is a huge irritant to empath children.

Short of keeping your child locked up in the house, there is no way to avoid exposing your child to loud noise. There are some things you can do to reduce his or her discomfort.

Let them wear earmuffs or earplugs. Earmuffs are great for blocking out sound, and there are plenty of fun looking earmuffs and earplugs that your child will enjoy wearing. If you are going to a noisy event, take a pair with you to drown out the sound.

Encourage your child to take breaks. When taking your child to a noisy event such as a family gathering, as well as wearing earplugs, you can also take him or her outside for a break when it appears that things are getting a bit too much. This will help them settle down so they can go back and enjoy the rest of the event.

Disliking people or being in certain environments: You might think that your child is rude because there are some people that they are just not able to tolerate. This may come in the form of them refusing to say hello or running from them when they come to the house. Do you dread taking your son or daughter to certain places because you know they are going to start acting up? That's because they don't like the environment because there is negative energy and bad vibes that they are unable to handle.

Empaths have very strong intuition, and they automatically know when something is not right. If they don't like one of your friends or a family member, trust their judgment and distance yourself from the person. It will probably save you from problems in the future.

If your child doesn't like being in certain environments, don't force them to go there. It will only make your kid anxious and depressed, and you wouldn't want to be responsible for upsetting them.

CHAPTER 16:

A STEP BY STEP GUIDE TO LIVING YOUR LIFE AS AN EMPOWERED EMPATH

L et's face it, living life as an empath is difficult, and there are many ways to ease any issues that may arise. If you want to embrace your gift and live life as an empowered empath, here are some suggestions you could incorporate into your daily routine.

Some of these steps have already been mentioned throughout the book, but there is no harm in being reminded of them. Remember, you are more powerful than you think, and you can tap into that power through consistent practice.

Love thy self: Yes, it might sound cliché, but before you do anything else, you need to focus on loving yourself. I want you to put your gift to the side for one moment and concentrate on loving you for you. Whether you want to accept it or not, you are a person before you are an empath and that's what you need to focus on. Think about when you first meet someone. Unless they are an empath, they are not going to know you are an empath. Once you get to talking and they decide that they like you, they will do so because of your personality, and maybe the things that you have in common and nothing else.

Empaths can be more insecure than the average person because they are so different. This will hinder your ability to live an empowered life. So here are some tips to help you love yourself a bit more.

What have you achieved? Accomplishments are an essential part of life, but sometimes we do not give ourselves enough credit for them. Get a pen and paper, sit down in a quiet place, and write down everything you have achieved in life. There is no time limit on this exercise. If you can remember something from when you were three years old, write it down.

What do you like about yourself? Most people don't think about this because we are so focused on what other people like about us. But when you realize that there are actually things that you like about yourself, you will start loving yourself more.

Get clear on your goals. There is nothing worse than having no purpose in life. Years go by, and before you know it, ten years have passed and you haven't achieved anything. However, when you know what you want out of life, and you are intentional about getting there, you won't feel so hopeless, which will help you love yourself more.

Spend time alone. Empaths are so focused on everyone else that they forget about themselves. They are constantly basking in other people's energy, and the majority of the time that energy is negative. Take time out each day to saturate yourself in your own energy.

Eat healthy foods. Food should be a very important part of an empath's life. Food is energy, and the more junk food you eat, the more you are surrounding yourself with negative energy. Consume a plant-based diet, eat lots of fruits and vegetables, and drink a lot of water.

Use crystals. Empaths function at their best when they are surrounded by high vibrational energy. Crystals can help you achieve this. You can either wear them around your neck or carry them with you in a small bag. Some crystals are better than others—choose those that hold the highest vibrational energy, such as:

- Black tourmaline prevents negative energy from coming into your field, and it is good for grounding.
- Labradorite protects your aura and blocks negative energy from draining you.
- Rose quartz helps you to love yourself more and emit a high love frequency.

Meditate. Meditation helps you to connect with yourself. It calms the mind and the soul, allowing you to connect with your spirit guides to get the help that you need.

Set boundaries. Empaths are terrible at setting boundaries. They find it extremely difficult because not only do they feel responsible for other people's happiness, they don't like to offend people. However, it is important to set boundaries as an empath to prevent burnout.

Practice self-awareness. The more self-aware you become, the easier it will be to discern when you are tapping into someone else's energy. You all know that dreaded feeling, one minute you are fine and the next you feel anxious, worried, scared, or depressed. The good news is that it doesn't have to paralyze you. Take some time out and acknowledge the fact that these feelings don't belong to you. Do a self-check, and whatever you are feeling ask yourself if it is justified. If not, you know it has come from someone in your environment.

Invest wisely. Just as in the finance world, there are good and bad investments, and the same principle applies to your life. There is nothing wrong with extending a helping hand, but there are some people who refuse to listen, won't take your advice, and will continue to do what doesn't benefit them. You should feed such people with a long-handled spoon or they will drain your energy.

Stay away from parasites. Unfortunately, empaths attract the wrong kind of people. Because you are so kind, open, and sensitive, you attract people who will manipulate, use you, and don't have your best intentions at heart. When you meet someone for the first time and something just doesn't feel right, trust your instincts and stay as far away from that person as possible.

Establish a morning routine. And last but not least, establish a good morning routine. Consistency is the key to living as an empowered empath. You want certain behaviors to become the norm for you. The only way this will happen is if you practice them daily. Here are some ideas.

- Wake up early, ideally between 5 am and 7 am
- Meditate for 10 minutes
- Journal, write down any dreams if you had any
- Read or listen to something positive
- Focus on your goals by going over your vision board
- Say some affirmations
- Write a to-do list
- Exercise
- Have breakfast
- Shower
- Go to work

Well, that's all folks, now it's time to get to work, remember – the more you focus on these steps and put them into practice, the stronger you will become!

CONCLUSION

have made a deep connection with my inner desire to become a blessing to the world, to push humanity to become all they were created to be. One of the reasons I wrote this book was to use my experience and abilities to help as many people as possible to live happy, fulfilled, and spectacular lives. This desire has manifested in ways that I could not have even dreamed of. When I think about everything I have accomplished in such a short amount of time, I am completely blown away.

So, let me ask you, what impact do you want to have on the world? What gifts and talents can you use to fill a void in someone's life? Please understand that when you are living your best life, you bring light to everyone who crosses your path. By embracing who you were destined to be, by living a blissful and dynamic life, you inspire the people you are surrounded by to do the same. Being your authentic self is one of the most important keys to successfully living life as an empath. I want you to be empowered, embrace your gift, and live a life that brings joy and abundance to the world!

THANKS FOR READING!

I really hope you enjoyed this book, and most of all got more value from it than you had to give.

It would mean a lot to me if you left an Amazon review – I will reply to all questions asked!

Simply find this book on Amazon, scroll to the reviews section, and click "Write a customer review".

Or alternatively please visit www.pristinepublish.com/empathnarcissistreview to leave a review.

Be sure to check out my email list, where I am constantly adding tons of value. The best way to currently get on the list is by visiting www.pristinepublish.com and entering your email.

Here I'll provide actionable information that aims to improve your enjoyment of life. I'll update you on my latest books, and I'll even send free e-books that I think you'll find useful.

Kindest regards,

Judy Dyer

ALSO BY
Judy Dyer

Grasp a better understanding of your gift and how you can embrace every part of it so that your life is enriched day by day.

Visit: www.pristinepublish.com/judy

NARCISSIST

a **COMPLETE GUIDE** *for*
DEALING WITH NARCISSISM
and **CREATING** *the* **LIFE YOU WANT**

JUDY DYER

CONTENTS

INTRODUCTION

Y ou will hear the word "narcissism" touted about as if it's
the latest fashion statement; however, what some people
don't realize is that it's actually a serious psychological
disorder that seriously affects the individual and the people who
are exposed to this vicious personality type. A study conducted
by the San Diego State University concluded that it is possible
that there is an "epidemic of narcissism" among the youth in the
United States. The researchers determined that celebrity culture,
permissive parenting, and the internet have all contributed to
this phenomenon. ABC News filmed a news story entitled "The
Rise of Narcissism in America," and psychologist Dr. Jean M.
Twenge wrote a book based on the San Diego State University
study, which highlighted that over the last two decades there has
been a 67 percent increase in narcissism. She also estimated that
approximately 10 percent of the population suffers from narcissistic personality disorder (NPD).

The bad news is that there is a high possibility that you are
working with, living with, or in a relationship with someone
who has some level of NPD. Even though this is unsettling, the
good news is that you are not alone in this situation and neither
do you have to stay in it.

From Greek mythology to the psychology of the modern
world, our understanding of narcissism has developed immense-
ly. The condition has been considered untreatable for many
years; however, over the last forty years, mental health profes-

sionals have started to identify successful ways to treat and manage the condition.

*Disclaimer: You will notice that throughout this book, I refer to the
narcissist as a "he," this is for no other reason other than for the sake of
consistency. Although statistics do state that the majority of narcissists
are males, there are also plenty of narcissistic women.*

JOIN OUR SUPPORT GROUP

In order to maximize the value you receive from this book, I highly encourage you to join our tight-knit community on Facebook. Here you will be able to connect and share strategies with others dealing with narcissists in order to continue your growth.

Taking this journey alone is not recommended, and this can be an excellent support network for you.

It would be great to connect with you there,

Judy Dyer

To Join, Visit: www.pristinepublish.com/empathgroup

CHAPTER 1:

A NARCISSIST – HOW TO RECOGNIZE ONE

O nce upon a time, there lived a handsome young Greek man, he was a hunter and the son of Cephissus the river god. He had many admirers; all the women loved him and would throw themselves at him; however, he showed no appreciation towards them, only contempt and disdain. One day, while Narcissus was searching for food in the woods, Echo, the Oread nymph saw him and fell in love with him and started following him. Narcissus sensed that he was being watched and Echo revealed herself and attempted to hug him. He shoved her out of his way and told her to get out of his space. Echo was devastated, her heart was completely crushed and as a result, she ended up living as a wanderer in the woods for the remainder of her life, until she disintegrated and all that was left of her was an echo.

Nemesis was the goddess of revenge and retribution, and when she found out what had happened, she took Narcissus to a river and made him look at his reflection, he fell in love with himself but didn't realize that it was only a reflection. Once he came to the conclusion that there was nothing he could do about the love that he was feeling, he became depressed and killed himself.

The mythology of Narcissus is where the term narcissism originated; however, it wasn't coined until the end of the nineteenth century. The story is a reflection of how today's narcissistic relationship plays out. Narcissus was too concerned with himself to notice that someone genuinely wanted to love him, and Echo desperately wanted to be heard, only to be pushed to the side. There are several versions of the story, and in one of them, Narcissus is so prideful that when someone tries to love him, he is horrified. He hears what Echo has to say but shouts at her to be quiet. Just as in a relationship with a narcissist today, the woman will often aggravate her partner to anger when she says or does something that he doesn't agree with. Just as the mythological story reveals, a narcissistic person is destructive to himself and to those who have a desire to love him.

CHARACTER TRAITS OF A NARCISSIST

- Little to no compassion or empathy for the feelings, opinions, and thoughts of others
- Demeans and belittles others to enforce their superiority
- Self-absorbed in their own problems and thoughts
- Has no respect or regard for authority
- Finds it difficult to deal with criticism
- Exploits people to gain exceptionalism and power or to make themselves feel that they are better than others
- Prone to outbursts of rage
- Lies and distorts the truth to support their own interests, perceptions, and goals

- Incapable of admitting when they are wrong
- Extreme jealousy
- As well as being emotionally abusive, the narcissist is also capable of physically abusing their partner

There is absolutely nothing wrong with having high confidence levels. At the end of the day, if you don't love yourself, who is going to love you? Everyone wants to be admired by friends, family, and loved ones for the things that they have achieved. However, when loving thy self turns into an obsession, it's time to get a little concerned. Self-love can become so obsessive, that you act as if you are the only person who exists on the planet and you have zero compassion for others. This type of attitude leads to abuse and other destructive behaviors that are detrimental to the individual and those around them.

EXPLAINING NARCISSISM

In 1898, British psychologist Havelock Ellis was the first to tell the story of Narcissus as a description of pathological self-absorption. The terms "narcissistic" and "narcissist" were soon picked up by other psychologists, and the words were popularized after Sigmund Freud wrote a report on the condition in 1914.

There is more to narcissism than having an inflated sense of self and being conceited and egotistical. Yes, these are all unattractive qualities when they are in the extreme; however, true narcissism involves a maniacal pursuit of praise, ambition, and gratification. Those who suffer from the slightest degree of NPD can be arrogant, smug, and vain and have an unusually high level of self-esteem. This is their outward appearance, but deep down they are extremely insecure and feel as if they have little self-worth. They thrive off admiration from others, which is how they feed their belief that they are more important than anyone else. Psychologists refer to this as "narcissistic supply," and it is almost like a drug for the narcissist. They are addicted to receiving confirmation that they are indeed superior beings. Typically, narcissists don't have an empathetic bone in their body, which basically means that they don't have a care in the world for anyone apart from themselves.

There are different degrees of narcissism; in fact, psychologists believe that we are all slightly narcissistic. It is even possible that narcissism is required as a method of survival in the world today. Being a little egotistical can be beneficial; however, the behavior of a fully narcissistic individual is very destructive.

According to the Diagnostic and Statistical Manual of Mental Disorders, to be considered narcissistic, a person's behavior must fall into the following categories:

- They blow situations out of proportion and are incapable of putting things into perspective.
- The narcissist is unable to empathize with the feelings or thoughts of others.
- The narcissist is only concerned with their own issues.
- The narcissist has no respect for authority.
- Deep down the narcissist feels inferior and will compensate by doing everything they can to be seen as superior.
- The narcissist is incapable of receiving constructive criticism.
- The narcissist needs sexual admiration and is often an exhibitionist.
- The narcissist is vain, exploitative, and dependent on others.

To a certain degree, all people who have been diagnosed with NPD exhibit these traits. However, there are also other types of narcissistic behaviors. Since the 1950s, there has been a dramatic increase in the number of people who suffer from narcissism. During this time, therapists have noticed that there are variations in the condition, which have been divided into several categories. Narcissism in children is typically a result of learned behavior from their primary caregivers and can be unlearned. Therefore, psychologists are reluctant to diagnose children with NPD. Fully-fledged NPD only exists in adults and is treated differently; other types of narcissism include the following.

- **The Phallic Narcissist:** These are typically males who have a great love for themselves and their physical bodies. They strut like roosters and are very aggressive and athletic. They are exhibitionists who enjoy putting their bodies on display.

- **The Manipulative Narcissist:** They enjoy manipulating and influencing others. The manipulative narcissist feeds their need for power by manipulating, bullying, lying, and intimidating others.

- **The Paranoid Narcissist:** The paranoid narcissist suffers from a deep self-hatred; they project this onto others with extreme jealous behavior, and they are overly sensitive to criticism.

- **The Craving Narcissist:** Although narcissists are extremely egotistical, craving narcissists are very needy, demanding of love, emotionally clingy, and attention-seeking.

The most significant personality trait of a narcissist is grandiosity. This is not the same as boasting or pridefulness, it is an unrealistic inflated sense of self. If a person won't stop going on about how they were the MVP of their college basketball team at a dinner party, it might show that that individual is boastful, conceited, or even a little ill-mannered. This can be extremely annoying; however, it isn't narcissistic if it is true. But if the person did not even play on the team but sat on the bench all season, that is being grandiose.

MILLION'S SUBTYPES

American psychologist Theodore Million is renowned for his pioneering work in identifying personality disorders. In his work, he has included several subtypes to narcissistic personality disorder.

- **The Amorous Narcissist:** The main characteristic of the amorous narcissist is an obsession with seduction and erotica—this is a subtype of the manipulative narcissist. They use sex appeal and sex as a weapon for power and control. This illusion of power is not restricted to the opposite sex, they believe that they can also use it against the same sex.

- **The Elitist Narcissist:** Displays the same characteristics of the phallic narcissist but is also female.

- **The Compensatory Narcissist:** Compensates for their deep feelings of low self-esteem and inadequacy by using narcissistic supply. They seek to build up an image of high self-worth by creating an illusion of superiority.

- **The Unprincipled Narcissist:** This type of narcissism is characterized by deliberate deception and pathological lying to obtain narcissistic supply. They are typically abusive conmen who are unscrupulous and deceptive.

- **The Fanatic Narcissist:** They love themselves so much that they think they are on the same level of a deity. They battle with low self-esteem and try to cover it up with extreme delusions of grandeur.

NARCISSISTS, PSYCHOPATHS, AND SOCIOPATHS

Narcissists are often referred to as psychopaths or sociopaths, which is not entirely true, although they do share similar character traits. According to criminology and sociology professor Dr. Scott Bonn, psychopaths, and sociopaths suffer from antisocial behavior disorder. They both have a complete disregard for the law, are callous, refuse to accept responsibility for their actions, lack empathy, have no respect for the rights of others, can be exceptionally violent, sexually promiscuous, and shallow. Narcissists also share these traits.

However, psychopaths often have a long and varied criminal history, whereas narcissists have a tendency to commit psychological and emotional transgressions in the way they slander, sabotage, and devalue the lives of their victims. They are capable of showing guilt or remorse, whereas psychopaths and sociopaths are often incapable due to their lack of empathy and self-absorption. Brain scans have revealed that both narcissists and psychopaths have brain abnormalities. Narcissists show structural abnormalities in the areas of the brain that deal with compassion, and psychopaths in the areas that deal with guilt and moral reasoning.

Narcissists have an unhealthy need for validation, but sociopaths and psychopaths are not concerned with it. Narcissists take advantage of people they are threatened by, whereas sociopaths do so simply because they enjoy it. However, when it comes to the callous nature in which they treat people, they are very similar and get sadistic pleasure out of harming people. This is because they have a desire for power and control, and since they are unable to experience the full range of human emotions, they get their pleasure out of traumatizing their victims.

You Will Never Truly Know a Narcissist

One of the most important lessons you must learn about a narcissist is that you will never truly know who they are. This is because the person you see in front of you isn't who they are behind closed doors. The narcissist will present themselves as successful, kind, generous, an intimate partner, intelligent, and charming. They are typically very well-loved people. However, they reveal their true colors to their partners, which is when they become cruel, selfish, abusive, hateful, lacking empathy, and having a tendency to step outside of the relationship. They will do things like make up situations to make it look as if the partner is needy and insane.

One common misconception about narcissists is that they are all extremely successful, accomplished, and powerful, but this is not always the case. Some of them are not very successful and have perhaps failed at life, and this can make them quite vulnerable. Although they will put on a display of superiority to hide their deep-rooted feelings of insecurity. Whether they are ultra-successful or living on the threshold of poverty, narcissists come in all shapes and sizes.

You will also find narcissists in philanthropic and charitable positions; for example, you will find them working as pastors in churches and as social workers. They actually thrive on taking positions where they will be able to execute their power. You will find counselors and mental health professionals who suffer from narcissistic personality disorder. They intentionally take on these positions, pretending to be empathetic when they don't have a compassionate bone in their body so that they have access to more victims. No matter the profession or social status, narcissists are very dangerous people with zero empathy. They believe that they are entitled to what they are not entitled to and they have no desire to change their behavior.

NARCISSISTS – THE TRUE SELF AND THE FALSE SELF

The narcissist supply is a term used to describe the admiration and attention they get from their victims. They care nothing for the people they target, and they target people for one reason only—narcissistic supply. They need this because they are incapable of connecting with others emotionally. It is also a form of entertainment for them because narcissists have the tendency to get exceptionally bored. Nothing entertains them more than to watch others suffer.

The narcissist sees their victims as some sort of accessory, like a piece of furniture or a handbag. Because they are lacking in the full range of human emotions, they lack the ability to understand that the people they are hurting have desires, wants, and needs. They have a fear of intimacy because getting close to someone would expose their true and unbearable character. They are good at faking their emotions and will often turn on the waterworks with great ease. They have a chameleon-like character and can adapt to what they think the other person wants or needs. They do this for manipulation purposes only, so they can get what they want out of their victims. They have what is referred to as "cold empathy," a psychological condition where a person is capable of having an intellectual understanding of what a person is going through, but they don't connect with the feelings. Even when they cry and act as if they feel remorseful, they only do so to get out of taking responsibility for their actions.

When narcissists get into a relationship, they lure their partners in with a false sense of security and intimacy. Their characters are very attractive which is why they are able to rope people in the way they do. A study conducted in 2015 found that women who desire to get married are typically attracted to narcissistic type personalities due to their charming nature, ability to provide, and social status. Despite their reputation for being so destructive in relationships, they are still viewed as desirable partners.

To those on the outside looking in, the narcissist is the kindest, most generous, at times spiritual and in-touch person. It is only those closest to them—their victims—that see the true evil side of a narcissist. Similar to psychopaths and sociopaths, narcissists create a shield of a charming, alluring and sweet demeanor to trap their victims in a web of splendor. This is how they get away with their behavior—nobody is going to believe that they are capable of such heinous actions. The victims are even led to question their sanity because the narcissist is capable of easily switching from nice to nasty in the blink of an eye. This makes the experience for the victim even more traumatic because they are just not sure if what they are experiencing is real. The reality of the situation is that the evil side of the narcissist is their true self, and the nice side is the façade.

When narcissists are wearing their mask, they are capable of fooling anyone including highly intelligent, educated, and successful people. No one is perfect, but most people don't go out of their way to make other people's lives miserable, so you just don't expect other people to do that. Victims would rather believe in the mask and just hope that the narcissist is just having a bad day when they show their dark side. Accepting that someone is just wicked is a difficult thing to do. It can take a significant amount of time before the cognitive dissonance in a victim is resolved when trapped in this type of relationship. What happens is that the victim develops conflicting thoughts, feelings, and beliefs about the abusive partner who is basically living a double life. To resolve cognitive dissonance, the solution lies in accepting that the abuse is taking place as opposed to denying or rationalizing it, which is a common response when victims develop a bond with their abusers.

To begin the process of disentangling yourself from the stronghold of narcissist abuse, you must first accept that narcissists do not feel any type of empathy for their victims. They simply do not care how you feel. The only type of feeling they may experience is referred to as "narcissistic injury," this is the despair and rage they feel when they are criticized, or when a person threatens their false sense of entitlement and superiority. This gives them a desperate need to protect their false selves even more. What I am trying to say is that there is no point in attempting to make a narcissist feel any type of remorse because their brains are not wired to do so. They will do anything to protect who they really are, which is why it is a waste of time to try to get the narcissist to see things through your eyes. Their main aim is to protect their true character by any means necessary.

So how do narcissists manage to deceive people the way they do? The reality is that they are capable of taking on multiple different personalities to get what they want from their audience. They will become who you need them to become to get their supply of attention, praise, sex, money, or whatever else it is that they want from their victim. They are also very good at projection and do a very good job of convincing their victims that they are the crazy ones and that their perception of reality is inaccurate. Narcissists have mastered the art of manipulation so well that the victims manipulate themselves into believing that what they are experiencing, hearing, seeing, thinking, and feeling is wrong. They can make you believe that the nasty comment they made was just a joke and they didn't really mean it or that the affair they've been having for the past six weeks was just a one-off and that's not who they really are. Narcissists are pathological liars who twist reality as if it's a normal part of everyday life to mask the true nature of their sadistic agenda.

It is of no surprise that the victims of narcissist abuse are left feeling isolated and confused. Narcissists find it very easy to convince the rest of the world that they are perfectly sane, and they take great pleasure in calling anyone who challenges their false perception of reality "crazy." This is their favorite word, and they will use it to describe anyone who has a normal emotional reaction to their volatile and unstable behavior. Over time, this becomes a complicated form of psychological torture in which the victim is no longer able to trust their own reality and gets sucked into the false reality of the abuser.

ALCOHOL AND DRUG ABUSE

Narcissists are extremely co-dependent; all aspects of the disorder rely upon the resources of others. The desire they have to be idolized is like a physical addiction, so it only makes sense that they are prone to other types of addiction such as drugs, alcohol, shopping, gambling, and workaholism. The narcissist is no different from any other addict—they gain pleasure from the actions and behaviors that feed their narcissistic supply. When they are not able to get this supply from people, they turn to other sources such as alcohol and drugs. These substances not only provide feelings of pleasure, but they also provide an escape from reality. People with NDP will indulge in substance abuse as a form of escapism when their reality is not supporting their imagined sense of self-importance. Basically, when people are not giving them the attention they feel they deserve. Narcissists see their addictions as a way to disassociate themselves from the inferior people they are surrounded by.

Narcissists also feel that they have some type of superhuman ability to control their intake of drugs and alcohol; and when confronted, they will vehemently deny that they have a problem, possibly even more so than an addict that does not suffer with NPD. In their world, they have full control over the addiction and can give up any time they want to. As far as they are concerned, since in their mind they have superhuman ability, illicit substances do not affect them the way they do everyone else. Narcissists are prone to becoming addicted to drugs and alcohol for the following reasons:

- Narcissists need to be highly stimulated
- It is a self-indulgent and selfish act
- It makes them feel complete
- It provides feelings of well-being and power

Narcissists, alcoholics, and drug addicts are prone to the same emotions. They all have unquenchable needs, and there is often a large gap between grandiosity and reality. For narcissists, that is typically the gap between the false mask that they wear and the harsh reality of their lives. Alcohol and drug abuse are self-medication for people with NPD—it is how they handle the pain that is caused by this gap.

When a narcissist is addicted to substance abuse, it is impossible to treat the addiction without first treating the NPD.

EATING DISORDERS

There is a close relationship between narcissistic tendencies and eating disorders. People who suffer from eating disorders are obsessed with body image. The most common types are anorexia (complete starvation), bulimia (purging and binge eating), and purging (eating small amounts of food and then vomiting). All of which are compulsive and impulsive behaviors. Narcissists are impulsive and reckless and can develop an eating disorder for the same reason they become addicted to drugs and alcohol. They have a desire to wield some type of influence or power over an area of their lives. The International Journal of Eating Disorders published a study and found that out of the eighty-four women with an eating disorder, and the seventy women who did not have eating disorders, there was a significantly higher ratio of women in the eating disorder group who exhibited narcissistic tendencies such as grandiosity and entitlement.

It is not common for people diagnosed with an eating disorder to suffer from full-blown NPD; however, there are high numbers of patients with eating disorders who display narcissistic tendencies. Think about it through the lens of the original story: Narcissus fell in love with an image that was unattainable—himself. This is the same as the person with an eating disorder, they are obsessed with an image they can never obtain.

DESTRUCTIVE RELATIONSHIPS

In the Narcissists world, there is no such thing as a successful relationship. This strong belief is typically the result osf some early childhood trauma that resulted in feelings of abandonment, betrayal, or humiliation. To the narcissist, any type of emotional attachment to a person is doomed to failure. That means getting attached to a career, home, or even an idea is in the same league as getting attached to a person. They simply have a disdain to getting attached to anything or anyone. For this reason, the narcissist avoids any type of intimacy; they surround themselves with people who will feed their narcissistic supply but won't make any meaningful friendships or relationships where they experience any form of emotional attachment to a person.

It is virtually impossible to be in a relationship with a narcissist; they live in a bubble where all they can see is their own reflection. You can try as hard as you want to, but whoever the significant other is will never get inside that bubble. This leaves them feeling frustrated, hurt, and alone. Narcissists are unable to develop any sense of pleasure or security. The only thing they will emotionally invest in is that which they can fully control—themselves.

One of the major problems with narcissists is their refusal to change their behavior. No matter what problems they are causing at home or at work, or regardless of how many people are complaining about their behavior, they will refuse to acknowledge it and act as if the only person who has a problem is the one doing the complaining. When it comes to any type of disorder, including addiction, the first step to getting any help is admitting that you have a problem. If the narcissist refuses to admit that they have a problem, they will never be able to get the help that they so desperately need.

CHAPTER 2:

WHAT CAUSES NARCISSISM?

B abies are born selfish—it's natural. Their number one concern is getting their immediate needs met and that's it. They have zero understanding of other people's desires and needs. As they transition into their teenage years, this self-centeredness is still very much a part of their nature as they go through the battle to attain independence.

In order to care and protect themselves, children need to develop a healthy level of self-esteem, at the same time as being able to care about others to stay connected to society and family and avoid dangerous influences. When a child has a healthy level of self-esteem, it is an indication that a child feels that they are worthy and loved within their family and valuable to society. The essence of healthy self-esteem is not feelings of self-centeredness because the individual doesn't feel as if they need to trample on others to get their needs met.

There must be a transformation in childish self-centered behavior in order to experience sound mental health in adulthood. The ability to function effectively in a family, and in society is dependent upon the child's ability to gradually see other people's points of view and to experience empathy. So, an emotionally healthy child should eventually become sincere about the well-being of others. The inability to develop empathy as a child is a red flag that they may be at risk of developing a personality disorder in adulthood, and this includes narcissism.

Preteens don't have the mental capability to be manipulative, which is why mental health professionals are reluctant to diagnose NPD any earlier than the age of 18. However, there are certain behaviors in teenagers that indicate that they might be on their way to developing the condition in adulthood.

- Continuous bullying behaviors such as degrading, threatening, making fun of or scapegoating people, including their parents and other adults
- The desire to win regardless of who gets hurt
- Constant lying, they will lie about the lies they tell, blame others for their lies, refuse to accept accountability by attacking those that report them to their parents
- A high and unnatural sense of self-worth
- Determined to get their needs met over others
- An attitude of extreme entitlement that leads them to act as if they should be treated differently than anyone else, and that regardless of the circumstances, they should get what they want
- Aggressive responses to being wronged, criticized, or upset
- Constantly blaming others when things don't work out the way they want
- Less cooperative and more competitive

The bottom line is that NPD is a result of the family environment that a child was raised in. All children want the attention and the approval of their parents, and they adapt to their surroundings.

However, there are some home environments that are so destructive that the only way a child is capable of adapting is to become narcissistic. Here are a few scenarios to illustrate this.

WHEN THE PARENTS ARE NARCISSISTS

More often than not, narcissistic parents are going to raise narcissistic children. As we have discussed, narcissists are very high achievers and they will put the same pressure on their children to achieve. Therefore, they will only reward their children when they come first. In this scenario, one or both of the parents are typically "exhibitionist narcissists," and the rule in the household is *"there is no point in trying if you are not going to be the best."*

When you are the main character of the school play, you score the most home runs, or you are first in the race, you are showered with attention and praise. Anything less than the best, you are seen as a disappointment and a disgrace to the family. Each child has to prove that they are special, not once, but time and time again. No matter what you achieve, there is still additional pressure to achieve more. As one woman stated during my research, "When I got all A's on my report card, my dad asked why I didn't get an A+."

Children in such families don't feel secure, they know that one wrong move and the love they received the night before will be withdrawn. It's difficult for them to just enjoy being children. Instead of their parents supporting them to find out what they are the most talented at and encouraging them in those areas, they are only supported if they are high achievers. Their parents are not interested in who their children really are, they are only interested in who they want them to be and the type of behavior that will elevate the family's social status.

These parents are only interested in their bragging rights and boasting to their friends and family members about how great their children are.

Children who are raised in such households only feel secure and have a sense of self-worth when they are recognized as the best and most successful. The conditional love they received as children, and the overemphasis of success and social status in the home, leads them to develop a habit of chasing success and believing that this is what brings true happiness. David's life is an example of this.

David was a highly successful man who suffered from NPD. He decided to go to therapy because he knew that something just wasn't quite right. He wasn't passionate about anything; his life looked excellent on paper, but he was empty inside. He had lost himself and he didn't know how; although David was a high achiever, he no longer gained any pleasure from his achievements. He started out enjoying his career and his hobbies, but now he only lives his life to impress other people because he gets nothing out of it.

THE NARCISSISTIC PARENT WHO DEVALUES THEIR CHILDREN

In this situation the parent or parents are very dominating. They are always putting their children down and devaluing them. The parent gets angry easily, is always irritable, and has high expectations for the child that are very unrealistic. If there is more than one child in the family, the parent will praise one child and put the other down. The "good child" can quickly become the "bad child," and vice versa. Everyone in the family feels insecure, and the majority of their time is spent attempting to pacify the temperamental narcissistic parent.

If only one of the parents is narcissistic, the other one experiences the same fate as the children. They are belittled and devalued when they don't agree with the narcissistic parent. Children who are brought up in such households feel inadequate, humiliated, and angry and will react to their upbringing in a number of different ways.

The Defeated Child: These children give up on life and accept the labels that have been ascribed to them. During their teenage years, they end up becoming depressed and riddled with self-hate. To numb themselves of the shame they feel, they indulge in addictive behaviors such as drug or alcohol abuse, or they get addicted to the internet. They find it difficult to achieve anything in life because their childhood years were spent being told that they were worthless.

The Rebellious Child: The rebellious child will reject what they have been told by their parents and spend their lives trying to prove to the world, and especially to their parents that they are not the losers they were referred to as children. They become overachievers and they spend their lives trying to prove that they are special. However, no matter how successful they become, there is always that still small voice criticizing them for every mistake they make.

The Angry Child: They become extremely angry with their parents and the world. Anyone who even slightly resembles their parents becomes the target of their rage. These children are more likely to grow up and become malignant or toxic narcissists where achieving isn't enough, they have to be destructive as well.

We find an example of this type of narcissism in the film *Pretty Woman*. The actor Richard Gere plays a successful businessman who buys companies and then breaks them up. He has a love for destroying the hard work of the former owners because to him, they represent the father that he hated. After hiring a prostitute (Julia Roberts), he eventually falls in love with her and settles down. Even his choice of a love interest is narcissistic. Narcissists have a tendency to want to rescue people, and narcissistic men will only date women they feel they can save, or who are of a lower social standing than them.

The Golden Child: You will find that such parents are closet narcissists who don't enjoy being in the spotlight. To compensate, they put their children in the spotlight instead. The majority of the time the child is extremely talented and deserves the praise and adoration they get. However, the parents will often take it too far and idealize the child. This can lead to the child developing narcissistic tendencies later on in life.

UNCONDITIONAL VERSUS CONDITIONAL LOVE – THE EFFECTS

Everyone wants to be loved unconditionally for who they are. If children feel that their parents only love and value them because they are special, this can lead to insecurity. It is impossible to win all the time, there is always going to be someone else out there who is better than you in some way. Children whose parents idealize them end up believing that they are only worthy when they are being idealized, if not they feel as if they have failed at life.

How They Perceive Flaws and Shame: Children who are idealized become ashamed when they realize that they are not the perfect people their parents raised them to believe they were. They can't handle the fact that they have flaws like everyone else and so strive to be perfect in every area of their lives.

Unable to Identify Who They Really Are: These children are unable to get in touch with who they really are. They only focus on doing the things that will appease their parents and win their approval. They never spend any time exploring their true identity and discovering what their interests are and where their talents lie.

Occasionally, the golden child may resist their role and avoid becoming narcissistic. They actually feel embarrassed by the over the top praise they receive. The role that has been ascribed to them becomes somewhat of a burden. For example, one child of an overbearing excessive parent told his mother that he no longer wished to be a part of the circus and that he would like to live his life without having to live up to the expectations of his overachieving parents.

THE EXHIBITIONIST ADMIRER

The exhibitionist narcissist parent will reward their children with attention and praise as long as they remain subservient to and admire the parent. These children are trained how to be narcissistic, but at the same time, they are prohibited from being in the limelight. The role they play within the family is to worship the awesomeness of the narcissistic parent without ever being critical of them or trying to surpass them in greatness.

This is how closet or covert narcissists come about, the children learn that they are provided with the narcissistic supplies of praise and attention if they refrain from competing with their narcissistic parents. If they ever attempt to be openly acknowledged as special, these supplies are withheld. The value they are given is based on their ability to act as a crutch to the egotistical nature of the exhibitionist parent.

As adults, children who were raised in these families feel too vulnerable, exposed, and uncomfortable to be in the spotlight, so their self-esteem and narcissism issues are not as obvious to anyone who isn't close to them. Some take on the role and play it very well, ending up in a job supporting an overachieving exhibitionist narcissist that they have nothing but admiration for.

Catherine worked as a personal assistant for the CEO of a successful organization. She had total admiration for him, and her entire life revolved around serving him. Because of her association with such a high-status individual, she felt special, and she lived for any amount of attention and praise she received from him. Catherine kept every birthday and holiday card he had ever given her. Catherine was so in love with her job, as well as having narcissistic tendencies herself, that she never got married. Whenever she met a man who was interested in her, she would compare him to her boss and discount him as unworthy. After working with such a high-profile individual, she felt as if other men were too inferior to waste her time with.

THE BOTTOM LINE

If you are ever concerned that the person you have met may have narcissistic tendencies, ask about their childhood and what their parents were like. Once you get a clear picture of their home environment it won't be difficult to work out whether they have narcissistic tendencies or not.

CHAPTER 3:

GASLIGHTING – A FORM OF NARCISSIST ABUSE

One of the most harmful forms of emotional abuse is gaslighting. Narcissists love to use this to tear down their victim's self-confidence to the point where they believe that what they are experiencing is something they have made up in their mind. The aim of this type of manipulation is to disorient and confuse the victim so that they relinquish total control to the perpetrator. The more they can get their victim to doubt that what they are going through is real, the easier it becomes for the narcissist to take over the victim's life.

Gaslighting also eliminates the victim's desire and ability to challenge the abuser because every time they do, the narcissist manages to turn the tables on them so that they feel as if they are in the wrong. Eventually, the victim becomes so paralyzed by fear and doubt that they end up doing everything the narcissist wants them to. They end up losing all self-respect and literally become a puppet to their wicked and calculating master. Here are some examples of gaslighting.

Gaslighting in a Relationship

The most common use of gaslighting is when one partner uses it against another in a relationship. From the outside looking in, the relationship looks perfect, and that is the image that the couple will attempt to portray. The narcissist will start the abuse early. They might tell you they were going to do something on Tuesday, but then when you bring it up, they completely deny saying that they said Tuesday, and that is was Wednesday. This seems pretty innocent, maybe you just got your days mixed up. This is just the start of the relationship and you are really into them, so you let it slide. Looking at something like this in isolation may not necessarily mean you are being gaslighted, it could be that you either misheard or that they accidentally said the wrong day. However, if this type of miscommunication starts happening more often, you will need to start asking questions.

As time goes on, you will start to notice more inconsistencies in what they say. You might suggest going to a Chinese restaurant because they once said that Chinese was their favorite food. You will then get the following response, *"I don't think that would be a good idea babe, I can't stand Chinese, but I know a great Italian place we could try."* At this point, you will start to wonder whether you are going deaf, you were speaking to another person, or they suddenly grew an aversion to Chinese food because you know that is what they said! This is the narcissist's way of making you feel guilty that you are not paying attention when they speak.

As the gaslighting intensifies, the abuser will start to make you feel as if you are the one who is backtracking on what you have said. Depending on how long you have been dating, they may or may not bring this to your attention. If they do, the conversation is likely to go something like this:

You: *"My family is really excited you are coming to Christmas dinner, they are really looking forward to meeting you."*

Them: *"I thought we had agreed to wait a while before we meet each other's families?"*

You: *"We just spoke about this two days ago and you said you couldn't wait to meet my family, especially my little sister."*

Them: *"I said that I am looking forward to getting to know your family, but I also mentioned that I would like to wait another couple of months. You said you thought that was a good idea because you didn't want to rush things, but since you've gone and told them I'm coming, I better come because I don't want to embarrass you."*

By agreeing to come, they are trying to get you to think that they are accommodating you for the mistake that you made (even though you know you didn't make a mistake). Something else the narcissist will do is to respond to your questions or statements with a lie:

"I bought those shoes we spoke about the other day. Remember, you said I could borrow your credit card? I've just ordered them off Amazon."

In this example, they will make up a conversation that you never had, claiming that you said that they could have access to your finances when they needed to. They know that this conversation didn't take place, you know that this conversation didn't take place, but if you attempt to confront them about it, they will lie even more stating that they asked you when you were busy cleaning and you probably don't remember. This is the narcissist's way of getting you to doubt yourself so that they can take total control over your life.

When they can see that they are breaking you down, the narcissist will graduate from subtle deception to full-blown lies, they will start telling you that you did or didn't do something, or that you did or didn't say something. Maybe after asking if they were hungry, they said no and so you put some food in the oven. You go and take a shower expecting your food to be ready when you come out. Instead, you come downstairs to find your partner eating it. They will insist:

> *"I just put this chicken meal in the oven, go and check to see if there is another meal in there because I only saw one when I put this in there. Maybe you heard me turning on the oven and got mixed up that you were doing it."*

As fictitious as this sounds, it works because, in your innocence, you refuse to believe that someone is capable of making up such bold-faced lies. Every time it happens, your self-worth is diminished even further, and you start to question everything you tell yourself.

GASLIGHTING IN THE FAMILY

In a family setting, gaslighting will most likely take place between the parents and the children, with the parents being the perpetrators. Children are extremely vulnerable to this type of manipulation because they rely on their parents for guidance and direction in life. The child is often the recipient of aggressive behavior whether they have done something wrong or not. A typical scenario might involve the following.

School starts at 9 am but it's 9:10 am and no one has left the house yet. The child is too young to leave the house alone and so they are waiting on their parents. The parent will insist that the child is at fault.

"You are late for school now because of your constant messing around, why can't you just learn to behave yourself?"

It is normal for a child to get into trouble because they were playing about and ended up being late for school. However, if the child has done nothing wrong but they are constantly getting blamed for something that they haven't done, it teaches the child that they are just a bad child. This leads to insecurity, low-self esteem, and them living up to the image that their parents have painted of them. It is natural for children to push the boundaries that have been set by them by authority figures. They will do this with their parents and teachers; it is an important process that teaches children about accountability and self-control. Healthy parents will enforce reasonable limits, but some parents are so strict that the slightest indiscretion leads to severe punishment, or they will say things like:

"You are so badly behaved, I really don't know how to cope with you."

Saying things like this reinforces the belief that the child is not good enough and they can't do anything right. It also creates an unhealthy fear in the child and restricts their ability or desire to want to discover and explore who they are. Their own parents have labeled them, and the child now believes that this label is true.

When children are still getting to know themselves and understand their emotions, gaslighting can sow seeds of doubt and make them question whether their feelings are legitimate. In another scenario, the family cat may have died, and the child is crying openly because he is deeply hurt about the loss of the pet. Instead of comforting the child, the parent dismisses his feelings and says: *"I don't know what all those tears are for, you didn't even love the cat anyway. You are just pretending so you can get attention. Your behavior is appalling. I'm the only one who is really upset about this, not you."*

The gaslighting will change as the child turns into a young adult and then an adult. By this stage, they may have become aware that things in the home are not normal and that they are being manipulated. The parent or parents will adapt to the growth stages of the child. One way they might do this is to move away from outright denial that something was said or done and insist that things have been misunderstood or taken out of context. They will then begin to say things like:

"You have completely misunderstood what I was trying to say. That's not what I meant at all."

"Your story does sound very similar to what I said, but you've got it totally mixed up."

Ultimately, statements like this make the child believe that they have taken what their parents have said out of context and that they've got it wrong because of the way they have interpreted the conversation.

Romantic partners and friends will come and go throughout a child's life, but they will still attach importance to these relationships. Even though the parents can see that the child has developed an attachment to these people, they will try to undermine the relationships. The parents will use gaslighting to convince their children that their partners or friends don't really like them, and they will say things like:

> "You know your friends are only using you because you've got a car, they don't really like you."

> "Jason doesn't have true feelings for you, he's only settling because there's no one else at the moment. As soon as someone better comes along, he will leave you."

> "Sandra told me that your friends only invite you out because they know that no one likes you and they feel sorry for you."

> "Justin treats you like trash, why do you stand for such behavior, you need to get rid of him."

The child will then start to question whether what their parents are saying is true. Even though they know that their parent is a liar and a manipulator, they will find it difficult not to let these comments affect them. These seeds of doubt that have been planted could potentially destroy a relationship that means a lot to the child.

Earlier you read about how memories are used as a way of confusing someone in a romantic relationship, this is no difference in a relationship between a parent and a child. The only difference is that these memories are not preserved as well because the child was young when the incident took place. A narcissistic parent can take advantage of this situation and tell the child that the event didn't happen the way they think it did, and then twist the facts to their advantage. For example, the sibling might have gotten into trouble at school for being rude to a teacher, but the parent will switch it and say:

"You were such a terrible child when you were younger, I really suffered raising you. Remember when you screamed at Miss Hollingworth and the principal called me to the school? You made me so ashamed!"

The child might be confident that it wasn't them that got into trouble but because it was so long ago, there is a possibility that they might be wrong. If the child attempts to insist that it wasn't them and that it was, in fact, their brother or sister, the parent will swiftly tell them that they are wrong and remind them of how young they were at the time, so they couldn't possibly remember.

When the child becomes an adult, the narcissistic parent will use gaslighting in defense of their parenting skills, they will attempt to convince the child that they had the best upbringing possible.

Child: *"You hit me a lot when I was growing up."*

Parent: *"That's a lie, the only time I ever put my hand on you was when you were really bad and that wasn't often."*

Child: *"I remember differently."*

Parent: *"Well there is something wrong with your memory because you and your brother had the best upbringing. We used to go on vacation all the time, don't you remember?"*

Although these examples are of a parent and child relationship, gaslighting in a family can happen in any context. It can happen between siblings, aunts, uncles, cousins, grandparents, etc.

GASLIGHTING AT WORK

Whether you are dealing with a narcissistic colleague or boss, gaslighting at the workplace does happen. It is typically used as a tactic to maintain or to gain power, and it can drive you insane if you allow it to. Gaslighting at the workplace can take place in one or more of the following ways:

Your boss asks you to do something in the office, you agree to do it and complete the task. After reporting back to your boss to tell him you have finished the job, you are told:

"Didn't I tell you to do X? You have gone and wasted the whole day doing something that's totally insignificant to the project we are working on."

You are not stupid, and you know what you heard, so you get a little bit irate and try and explain that he is mistaken. You are then met with the following comment:

"Calm down, don't you think you are taking this a bit out of hand?"

Another scenario might be, your boss promised you a pay rise after six months, so you've spent the last six months working as hard as you can. You turn up to work before everyone else and leave later than everyone else. Sometimes you come in on weekends when your boss asks you to. So, you are in the seventh month and you decide to jog your boss' memory about the pay raise:

"I categorically didn't say you'd definitely be getting a raise. What I did say was that it was something I would consider based on your performance; and so far, I'm not impressed."

On the other hand, you have a colleague who will do anything to get a promotion before you. They will say some nasty things part way through a conversation just to knock your confidence and undermine your ability to get a higher position in the job:

> *"I hear that you might be in a bit of trouble, mate? The boss is fuming about the report you submitted; apparently, it's a load of rubbish! He says he wishes he gave it to me to write instead."*

> *"Didn't you get the email about xyz? Oh, I better not say anything then, you were probably kept out of it because the boss doesn't trust you with such sensitive information yet."*

> *"Oh my goodness, you really need to calm down, I only said you need to put a bit more effort into the job. Gosh, someone woke up on the wrong side of the bed this morning!"*

Additionally, narcissistic and manipulative employees might erase all the information off your hard drive when you go out to lunch. Or move things around when you know you left them in a certain location.

Remember, the main aim of gaslighting is to make you feel insecure and to confuse you. There are several different ways that this can happen.

THEIR SECRET WEAPON

In some cases, the narcissist will intensify the confusion by spending a certain period of time being evil. They will literally have the individual on the brink of walking out the door, then they will do a full 180 and become the kindest, most loving, and charming person ever. The aim of this is to keep the victim hoping that whatever happens, there is always going to be a positive outcome. They then start to believe that the relationship is not that bad after all and they can cope for another day. The side effect of this treatment is that additional seeds of uncertainty are sown into the mind of the victim. Up until this point, the victim has known what to expect, but now, they are not sure what side of the abuser they will see on any given day. This element is especially common in romantic relationships. The victim has such a warped concept of love that they are held in perpetual bondage to their abusive partner.

ADDITIONAL SIGNS TO CONFIRM YOU ARE BEING GASLIGHTED

The examples listed above might sound familiar to you. If that is the case, this extreme mind manipulation will have had a negative effect on your mental health. If you suspect that you might be a victim of gaslighting, here are some signs that you can identify within yourself that this is the case:

You Have Low Self Esteem

Your opinion of yourself is so low that you accept abusive treatment from your partner. Any confidence you once had in your abilities has been completely diminished, and you believe you deserve what is happening to you. These feelings of low self-worth lead you to turn down opportunities to progress in your career, to socialize, and to grow as a person. There is also the possibility that you experience anxiety because you feel as if you are unable to cope with small challenges.

Your Character Flaws are Your Main Focus

The main aim of a narcissist using gaslighting tactics is to make you feel as if you are not good enough and that you will never

be good enough. You will find that you spend copious
of time focusing on the things you think are negative about
you. In most cases, these will be personality traits that your
abusive partner has highlighted. You will start to believe that
you are inherently damaged or bad and that your flaws make
you unlovable or unlikeable. A narcissist will do this so that you
will feel that there is no point in leaving because no one else
will want you.

You are Always Questioning Yourself

Did you put the butter in the bread bin and the bread in the
fridge by accident? You better go and check just in case. The
confidence in your memory has been completely shattered to
the point where you find it difficult to function and always feel
as if you have done something wrong. The narcissist is happy
when they see you acting in this way, it means that you are easier to manipulate, they have managed to convince you that you
are crazy, they can deny anything and make up lies and you will
believe them.

You Find it Difficult to Make Decisions

You have become incapable of making even the smallest decisions alone. You don't have any confidence in your ability to
make the right choices, so in most cases, you will turn to your
abusive partner for help. This is a strategic move on their part,
they have placed themselves in a position to make you believe
that they are the solution to your problems. Again, there is less
chance of you leaving if you feel that you need your partner to
help you make basic decisions.

You Don't Feel Like Yourself Anymore

You feel as if there is someone else inhabiting your body, you have vague memories of the person you once were, and you are unable to recognize yourself. In a way, you feel as if you are looking back at a past life you once lived.

You Feel Like a Failure

Your self-esteem is so low that you feel like a failure, and you think that everyone else thinks you are a failure too. In your mind, you feel as if there is nothing good about you and that you are incapable of achieving anything in life.

You Are Constantly Apologizing

You feel that if there is a problem, it must be because of you. Regardless of whose fault it actually is, you always feel the need to apologize. This is exactly what the narcissist wants, it means that they will never have to take responsibility for their actions because you will always take the blame.

You Make Excuses for the Narcissist's Behavior

Sometimes your narcissist partner will slip up and treat you badly in front of friends or loved ones. Instead of chastising them, you are quick to defend their behavior and make excuses for them. In your mind they have every right to behave like that, you deserve to be treated in this way.

You Think You are Overreacting

One of the character flaws you see in yourself is that you are oversensitive. You believe that the only reason your partner gets so angry with you is because you overreact to the smallest thing. You think that if you could learn not to get so offended, things would be better for you.

You Avoid Confrontation by Lying to Yourself and Others

You hate confrontation because your partner always manages to defeat you and convince you that you are the one in the wrong. So, in order to avoid the most minor disagreements, you find yourself lying. Instead of saying no to things that are of no benefit in your life, you say yes. You don't question people when they make unreasonable demands from you. For the sake of maintaining peace, you will even act against your own morals and values.

Deep Down You Know Something is Wrong

Somewhere deep in your gut, you know that the relationship you are in is not right. The problem is that you have been blinded to red flags that would be clear to someone who hasn't had their mind manipulated. You are so confused that you can't work out what the issues are and so you are unsure of how to approach them. You always have the thought in the back of your mind that you are the person responsible for the mess you are in.

You Feel Nervous Around the Narcissist

Your entire body tenses up whenever the narcissist walks into the room. This is how the psychological and emotional abuse that you have endured manifests whenever you are in their presence. It is your body's way of preparing for further abuse.

You Can't See Any Way Out

Because of everything you are experiencing, you have resigned yourself to your fate. You don't think there is anything you can do to get out of your situation.

CHAPTER 4:

WHAT TO DO WHEN YOUR PARENT IS A NARCISSIST

A narcissistic parent is one who is described as living their lives through their children, overly possessive, or they marginalize their children and compete with them. In general, the narcissistic parent is threatened by their child's independence, even in adulthood. They force their children to live in their shadow, placing unrealistic expectations on them. Parents of narcissistic children are unable to love their children for who they are.

The majority of parents want to be proud of their children, they desire to show them off, they expect them to do well in school, and will be firm when they are displaying destructive behaviors. These are not traits that characterize pathological narcissism. However, the main characteristic of a narcissistic parent is a tendency to deny their children the right to become independent, even in adulthood. The parents believe that the sole purpose of the children is to serve their needs. If you suspect that one or both of your parents are narcissists, here are some signs that your suspicions are correct.

Marginalization: Despite the narcissist's inflated ego, in general, they are extremely insecure people and have a tendency to feel threatened by anyone who has the potential to steal their shine, including their own children. The result of this is that the narcissistic parent will do everything in their power to put the child down so that the parent can maintain their status of perceived superiority. They will do things like compare their children unfavorably to others, nit-pick, criticize and judge them unreasonably, and reject their accomplishments and success. They will say things like, *"You will never be good enough,"* or *"You've always got issues."* By lowering the child's self-esteem, the parent elevates their own self-worth.

During therapy, one girl stated that she begged her mom for money to pay for the lab fee for a science class in college. She agreed to pay for it but reminded her that because she was spending the money on her, she may as well have been burning it.

Lives Through or Uses the Children: The majority of parents want their children to be successful; however, the difference between a narcissistic parent and a normal parent is that they want the child to succeed for their own benefit, so they can say *"Look at what my child has achieved."* Such parents fail to nurture the goals, emotions, and thoughts of the child. The child becomes an extension of the parent's personal desires and is not allowed to become his or her own person.

> *"Even though I was a tomboy, and I hated dressing up like a girl, my mum used to make me wear these cute frilly dresses. I think she felt that when people complimented me, it made her look good and boosted her self-esteem."*

NARCISSISTIC PARENTS WILL MAKE COMMENTS SUCH AS:

"My son better play for the NBA when he grows up or I'll kill him!"

"Oh, you are such a beautiful little girl, you are going to grow up to be just as stunning as your mother."

"I never had the opportunities that you had when I was growing up, so until you become a lawyer, you are going to do what I tell you."

Superiority and Grandiosity: Most narcissistic parents have an inaccurate inflated self-image. They don't treat people like human beings but as tools used for personal gain. Children of narcissistic parents are treated in the same way, or some are taught to feel as if they are superior to others and that people are simply objects to be disposed of once they have been used. This grandiose sense of entitlement is achieved by diminishing humanity.

Manipulation: Narcissistic parents who manipulate their children often do so in one or more of the following ways.

Shaming: *"Your inability to achieve is a disgrace to the family."*

Blaming: *"I wish you were never born; you are the reason why I am not happy."*

Guilt trip: *"You are so ungrateful, after everything I've done for you in this world."*

Unreasonable Pressure: *"You WILL get an A and make your parents proud."*

Negative Comparison: *"Why can't you be as clever as your sister?"*

Manipulative Punishment and Reward: *"If you don't go to college to become a doctor, I won't financially support you through your studies."*

Emotional Coercion: *"Unless you are able to meet my expectations, you are not a good child."*

The common thread that runs through this type of manipulation is conditional love. I will only love you if you do this, and I will withdraw my love if you do that. They are incapable of expressing healthy parenting skills.

Superficial Image: Some narcissistic parents enjoy showing the world how amazing their family is. They take great pleasure in publicly parading what they think they have that is superior to others, whether it's physical appearance, material possessions, accomplishments, projects they are a part of, memberships to a specific club, a trophy wife or husband, good looking children, or connections to people in high places. Whatever it is, they do their best to seek flattery and attention. For a lot of narcissistic parents, social media is a dream come true, as it gives them the opportunity to post pictures of their supposedly perfect lives with the underlying message being *"My life is so wonderful, look what I've achieved!"*

"The image that my mother displays in public is nothing like the person she really is."

Touchy and Inflexible: Some narcissistic parents are very rigid when it comes to how they expect their children to behave.

Every minor detail is regulated, and when the child steps outside of those boundaries, all hell breaks loose. There are many different reasons a narcissistic parent will become irritated with their child. It may be because they are not paying enough attention, they are not doing what they have been asked, or the parent may feel as if they fall short in certain areas. It can even be as simple as being in the parent's presence at the wrong time. One of the reasons for this type of touchy behavior from the parent is a desire to control the child, and when they are not able to control the child's every move, the parent reacts in rage.

"I can't stand it when you arrange the cans in the cupboard that way, I have told you before I HATE IT."

Dependency/Co-dependency: There are some narcissistic parents who expect their children to take care of them for the rest of their lives, whether it is physically, financially, or emotionally. Although there is nothing wrong with looking after your parents, especially when they get older, the problem is when the narcissistic parent manipulates their children into doing so and makes unreasonable demands on them with total disregard to the needs of their children.

"My mom is a single parent; she demands that I take care of her financially or she won't be able to survive."

Possessiveness and Jealousy: Narcissistic parents hope that their children will always live under their influence. When the child begins to mature and become independent, the parent becomes exceptionally jealous and possessive. This independence can take the form of making their own friends to choosing their own academic or career path. Such behavior is interpreted negatively and taken personally. In particular, a romantic partner becomes a huge threat to the parent, so they often respond with criticism, rejection, and competition. The narcissistic parent doesn't believe that any partner, no matter how well they treat their child is good enough.

"How dare that man take my daughter away from me! Who does he think he is?"

Neglect: There are some narcissistic parents who just leave their children to get on with it. Their main concern is themselves and they are too self-absorbed to care about what their children are doing. Whatever activities they are participating in provides the narcissist parent with the stimulation, validation, and feelings of self-importance that they crave. This could be in the form of hobbies, a career, personal adventures, or social flamboyance.

"My husband is never at home, he is basically an absent father, he is always off doing something that he enjoys rather than spending time with our child. He is a very selfish individual."

One of the most common characteristics of a narcissistic parent is a lack of empathy. The parent has no consideration for the child's thoughts and feelings, and the only thing that's important to the parent is how they think and feel. Children who are raised in this type of environment will do one of several things to survive. They will either stand up for themselves and fight back, they will distance themselves, or some will develop a false persona to deal with the pain of who their parents have caused them to be. In this way, they are developing narcissistic characteristics.

My Parent(s) are Narcissists – Now What?

So, you've worked out that one or both of your parents are either full-fledged narcissists or they have narcissistic tendencies. Regardless of the situation, you have a right to live a normal and healthy life no matter what your parents are doing. You may feel as if you need to help them, but the truth is, it's not your responsibility. Even if you are still living under your parents' roof, there are several ways you can help yourself.

Learn About the Condition: The more you know about narcissism, the easier it will be for you to navigate your situation. There are plenty of books and resources on the internet that will give you more information about the condition.

Accept That Your Narcissistic Parent Might Never Change: One of the main character traits of a narcissist is that they refuse to accept responsibility for their actions. They will never admit that they are wrong and as you have read live in their own little world of self-importance. As much as you love your parents and you would like them to change, this is not something you can encourage them to do. A lot of children of narcissistic parents hope that their parents will one day love them for who they are. Unfortunately, unless your mother or father accepts that they have a problem, which may never happen, they will never get the help that they need, and you will never experience the love that you have craved your entire life.

Recognize That One of Your Parents is an Enabler: If one of your parents is a narcissist, the other parent is the enabler. Enablers excuse the behavior of the narcissist, which leads to normalizing and sustaining the behavior. Sometimes the enabler also assists their narcissist in their exploits by perpetuating and condoning the abuse. The enabler is often a victim of the abuse, but by refusing to call it out when it's happening to the child, the other parent is indirectly participating in the abuse.

Sometimes it is even more difficult to forgive the enabling parent than the narcissistic parent. This is because you know that the enabler is sane, and they really don't have any excuse for not protecting you. This can lead to terrible feelings of betrayal.

Understand the Family Roles: What is the role you play in the family, are you the golden child? Have you ever been the enabler? In a narcissistic family, the roles are often fluid, but this depends on the agenda of the narcissist. You may have been the golden child and the angry child because the narcissist controls the family by utilizing the divide and conquer strategy. As a result, you may feel alienated from your siblings (if you have any), and from your other parent. There is also the possibility that you feel as if they have betrayed you. However you might be feeling, it is important to remember that all family members are a part of a twisted system that has been constructed by the dominant narcissist in the house with the sole purpose of serving their needs to the detriment of others. Each one of you has had to fight to survive after being forced into your perspective roles.

A united front is the most powerful defense against the narcissist. If you are on one accord with the rest of the family members, this is the easiest way to put an end to narcissist abuse. However, if this is not the case, your next course of action is to defend yourself against the narcissistic parent.

Set Boundaries: This will infuriate the narcissist, but you have to be strong and continue to enforce them. Narcissists enjoy violating boundaries; they believe that they own their children and it is their right to control and manipulate them. If you are the golden child, your job is to live the way your parent wishes they could have lived, and then project this false image to the world. Regardless of your role, the child of a narcissist is objectified and their identity as a person is ignored. The narcissist decides how you are supposed to think and feel and demands that you comply with their version of reality. If you don't, you will have to suffer the consequences. One of the hardest things you will have to do is establish healthy boundaries.

Get in Touch with Your Feelings: Children of narcissistic parents have been indirectly trained to deny their feelings. In the house, they are not important and the only person that matters is the narcissistic parent. Your feelings are threatening to the narcissist because more than likely, they are going to conflict with the needs, demands, and beliefs of the narcissistic parent. Your feelings are denied through shame, ridicule, rage, and other forms of attack, which lead you to hate or even fear your feelings. One of the most important things you can do for yourself as a victim of narcissist abuse is to reconnect with your feelings. You may feel as if you don't have any because you have had to suppress them for so many years, but they are there. Allow yourself to feel your emotions, treat them with respect. You will find yourself in your feelings and maneuverer your way out of the web of splendor that you had been en-trapped by. Your parent(s) have violated you and hurt you in the worst possible ways, and you will have to work your way through these feelings of extreme pain and anger. The majority of narcissists project their inability to feel any emotions onto others, they will even go as far as accusing them of the same abusive behavior they are displaying. So, when you first start this process, you will find it difficult to differentiate between your own feelings and the ones you have been brainwashed to believe. Be patient with yourself as you learn to reconnect with your feelings again.

Stop Harming Yourself: People raised in narcissistic families are prone to self-abuse. Since they have been indirectly trained to hate themselves, they are prone to indulge in self-punishing, self-destructive, and thrill-seeking behaviors such as substance abuse. If you fall into this category, you are internalizing the abuse you were exposed to. By harming yourself in this way, you are allowing your narcissistic parent to yield the same power over you as they did when you were a child. You will also make the psychological and emotional trauma you were forced to endure worse. Patterns of addiction and self-harm can be difficult to break, so it is important that you get professional help to assist you with this.

Be Aware of Your Attraction to Narcissists: To add insult to injury, children who experienced narcissist abuse grow up to attract narcissists as partners, friends, and managers. This is not a nice thing to have to deal with; however, if you have fallen victim to narcissist abuse in adulthood, you simply have to learn from your mistakes and move forward. This is one of the main reasons it's important to educate yourself about narcissism. It will help you to develop a high-powered radar against narcissists so that you can protect yourself against them.

Accept How You Feel About Your Narcissist Parent: All children love their parents, in most cases, regardless of what they do. They want love, adoration, and attention from their parents. Unfortunately, the narcissistic parent is incapable of loving their children the way they deserve to be loved. Combined with anger and grief, you may also feel sorry for your parent. There is also the possibility that you have no feelings for your parent because you have been too abused to love anymore.

Regardless of how you feel, try not to be too harsh on yourself for it, acknowledge your feelings and allow them to guide you in the way you interact with your family. If you feel like the safest choice is to break contact with them, then that is what you should do. Or be strict with your boundaries and lower your expectations. Unless narcissist parents are totally sadistic, some of them are capable of showing their children affection, even if it doesn't really come from the heart. It may not be often, but they will do so sometimes, so when it's there, take it.

Cleanse Yourself of Narcissistic Fleas: When you are raised by narcissistic parents, there is a high possibility that you are going to pick up some of their traits. These are referred to as "narcissistic fleas," and nobody wants fleas, and you definitely don't want to end up like your narcissistic parent(s)! The good news is that you can avoid this if you are aware and mindful of your situation. The fact that you have already come to the realization that your parent(s) is a narcissist is a good starting point. Now it is your responsibility to ensure that you don't take on the same characteristics. Examine yourself thoroughly, what are your triggers? Is there anything you do that reminds you of your narcissistic mother or father? Do you have a bad temper? Do you use manipulation or guilt to gain control and seek attention? Are you sensitive to the needs and perspectives of others?

We don't have any choice in how we were raised, but we can choose how we react to it. Being brought up in a narcissistic household is very traumatic and no child should have to live with that. Unfortunately, we can't choose who our parents are, we simply have to make the most of what we have. The best revenge in life is success, so instead of allowing your bad upbringing to destroy you, allow your pain to propel you into your purpose in life.

CHAPTER 5:

EMPATHS AND NARCISSISTS – THE TOXIC COUPLE

O pposites attract is a statement that most people have heard all their lives. While this saying has the potential to get you to step outside of your comfort zone and interact with people that you normally wouldn't, it can also be pretty dangerous.

As you have read, narcissists are attracted to people they can use; and empaths are often their main targets. Empaths and narcissists are complete opposites. Narcissists don't have any empathy and live for admiration. Empaths, on the other hand, are in tune with other people's emotions and are extremely sensitive. They are like emotional sponges and absorb the energy of the people around them. These character traits appeal to narcissists because they see empaths as people who will selflessly cater to their needs.

A TRAIN WRECK WAITING TO HAPPEN

A relationship between an empath and a narcissist will never work out. Narcissists are attracted to empaths because they see them as loving, giving people who are going to be totally devoted to them. Empaths are attracted to narcissists because of the false image that they portray; they appear to be extremely charming, giving, and intelligent until you don't do what they say and their true cold nature comes out. When a narcissist wants to hook someone, they will be attentive and loving, but that mask will soon disappear. At the start of the relationship, they only see the good side of the narcissist, sparks will fly, and the empath will feel as if they have found the love of their life. This doesn't last very long because narcissists are full of hatred and they believe that everyone is beneath them. Once the narcissist starts to notice that the empath has flaws, they stop idealizing them and start victimizing them for not being perfect. Not only that, but they begin to resent the empath's natural ability to empathize with people. They start getting frustrated and lashing out at the empath for being too dramatic or sensitive. Suddenly, their emotions are no longer an asset but a flaw.

What makes a narcissist turn so quickly? The narcissist loves being admired, and once he's got everything he needs, he no longer has a need for the empath and starts to pull away. But the empath won't leave, they will wait around for the narcissist to need them again and the cycle continues. It is difficult for an empath not to fall in love with a narcissist because it goes against their instincts. They believe that they can fix people and heal them with compassion. Empaths find it difficult to believe that a person is incapable of showing empathy.

NARCISSISTS LOVE CHAOS AND DRAMA

Empaths will do anything for peace and harmony, whereas narcissists love chaos and drama and enjoy pulling people's strings. They enjoy manipulating empaths by leading them on with intermittent hope. They will incorporate kindness and compliments into their behavior and lead the empath to believe that if they behave in the right way, they will get the kind and loving person back that they first met. Empaths believe that all humans make mistakes and so they are willing to be patient with people they think are struggling with personal development. If a narcissist tells an empath that they want to change, an empath will stick around waiting for it to happen. Narcissists have a strategy they use where they will admit that they've got issues, but they don't follow through with making changes. This is how they reel the empath back in, and it works with them because they want to help their partner grow and support them. Because empaths are naturally caretakers, they can sense that the narcissist has an underlying problem and they desperately want to fix it. However, what they are unable to see is that the narcissist lives to take from people, and they will feed off them like an energy vampire. The more attention the narcissist is given, the more victimized and drained the empath will become.

WHEN THE RELATIONSHIP BECOMES TOXIC

The narcissist is driven by ego—they live for the love and attention shown to them by the empath. After a while, they realize that they get more attention from the empath when she is in the narcissist's bad books. At this point, they will begin to manipulate and engineer situations, and it is at this stage that the relationship starts to become emotionally abusive. The narcissist will introduce an element of control to enable him to dominate the relationship. They will start casually dropping demeaning and destructive comments so that the empath doesn't step out of line. Sensitive people can't handle being told they are not good enough, so they start thinking that if they try harder or love them a bit more things will go back to normal. Unfortunately for the empath, that's exactly what the narcissist wants. They want you to keep giving more, but your more will never be enough—EVER! The narcissist will keep taking, and the empath will keep giving until they don't have anything left to give.

At this point, one of two things will happen: The empath will get so emotionally drained that they can no longer provide narcissistic supply, and the narcissist then gets bored and leaves the relationship because she is no longer feeding him. Or the empath will get an epiphany, realize what's going on and leave. Either way, the relationship is destined for failure—it will never work and there is no point in trying to force it.

EMPATHS AND TRAUMA BONDING

Empaths will typically form a trauma bond with their narcissistic partner. The push and pull nature of the relationship leads to the victim feeling as if it's impossible to leave the relationship, no matter how much damage is being caused. Narcissists take advantage of the empath's willingness to look at themselves and acknowledge their faults, which becomes a vicious cycle for the empath. Due to the intuitive nature of the empath, they can typically sense that their partner is a narcissist and that they are not really capable of having a genuine love for them. However, due to the abusive nature of the relationship, it becomes extremely difficult to break free from the cycle of destruction and attraction. Anytime she is hurt for whatever reason, the empath becomes isolated because the narcissist is unable to comfort her.

IT WILL NOT GET BETTER

It is essential that the empath understands that the narcissist is so wounded, there is nothing she can do to fix him. The relationship is never going to get better, it is only going to get worse. The empath does not have the ability to empathize and must exit the relationship before her self-esteem and energy are worn down any further. Since the narcissist doesn't have any empathy and the relationship benefits him because of the ample narcissistic supply he is receiving, he will never put an end to the relationship. Therefore, the empath must find the strength to get out quickly before it is too late.

How to Avoid Getting into Another Relationship with a Narcissist

Narcissists are extremely charismatic, and it's difficult not to get caught up in their charm. If you are not aware, it can be difficult to single them out because they are so skilled at camouflaging themselves. They are social chameleons, and they know exactly how to manipulate your feelings with what they say. It is important that sensitive people are aware that they are easy prey for narcissists, but they should never confuse this with being powerless. Here are some tips to assist you in avoiding narcissists.

Know Who You Are: When you know what you stand for and what you will and won't accept, the narcissist, or any other person for that matter, will have a difficult time convincing you that you don't deserve to be in a healthy relationship. Having the ability to tune into the emotions of others is a powerful gift, it is something that makes you an awesome and amazing person. However, spend some time alone and tune into your own feelings to get an idea of who the person pursuing you really is.

Recognize the Red Flags: As mentioned, narcissists know how to hide who they really are. However, they will reveal themselves if you look hard enough. Empaths have a habit of ignoring people's bad characteristics because they think every human being is deserving of compassion. However, there are some things that should not be overlooked.

- He's Possessive: You've just met him, but he has a problem with you having friends or wanting to spend time with your family.

- You Never Look Good Enough: At the beginning of a relationship, a narcissist will never directly tell you that you don't look good in what you are wearing. However, he will make suggestions and say things like, "I think you look better in black."

- They Are Rude to Other People: He might be as nice as pie to you because he is trying to reel you in, but he treats everyone else like something off the bottom off his shoe! This is a real indicator of his true character.

- He Speaks Badly about His Ex: Some relationships just don't end well and that's life. However, if he is constantly insulting his ex, and blaming her for everything that went wrong in the relationship, he has got some serious issues.

- He's Controlling: Possessive and controlling are two completely different things. Someone of a controlling nature is going to try to tell you what to wear, what to eat, how to sit, etc. Run away if you get a hint of such behavior.

CHAPTER 6:

WHY VICTIMS STAY – EMOTIONAL AND PSYCHOLOGICAL REASONS

Unfortunately, abusive relationships are extremely common; according to statistics, one out of every four women will be abused by a partner at some point in their lives. Abuse is also one of the crimes that goes unreported the most, which means that there are probably more cases of abuse than we are made aware of.

WHAT IS TRAUMATIC BONDING?

The biological process of bonding allows an emotional connection to develop between two people; normally, this is through a positive experience. The word "bonding" is generally associated with positive images of loving and intimate moments being shared by families and couples. The opposite of this is traumatic bonding where a bond is created between two people in an abusive relationship. The average person cannot understand why someone would stay with someone who hurts them, the answer lies in the psychological need to survive. Traumatic experiences cause us to shut ourselves off emotionally; numbness sets in, and in order to survive, our primal instincts kick in. One of the things the abuser does is subconsciously focus on the positive characteristics of the one being abused and ignore the fact that she has just had her two front teeth knocked out by the man who is supposed to love her. How many times have you heard a battered woman talk about the hell she is going through only to state, *"But, he's a really nice guy though."*

Trauma bonding is associated with The Stockholm Syndrome (TSS), a psychological disorder named after a hostage situation that took place in 1973. According to reports, the hostages formed an emotional attachment to their kidnappers. They stated that they were more afraid of the police who rescued them than the perpetrators. They even went as far as to set up a fund to help pay their legal fees!

Trauma bonding takes place through a process of conditioning that psychologists have referred to as the "arousal-jag." This is where the narcissist gives their victim something to make them happy and then takes it away. This is done strategically over and over again, and it is this that creates the trauma bond. The narcissist is connected to the feeling of the excitement that he or she experiences when they do what they do. This is one of the reasons narcissists have more than one partner—the excitement factor is intensified. The victim becomes attached to the chaos, and sadly they eagerly wait for it, and this is an additional bonus for the narcissist.

The narcissist takes their victim through a process of devaluing them—there is a period of neglect and betrayal. Just before they are about to get discarded, the victim feels a sense of loss, and the behavior of the narcissist indicates that they are going to leave. The victim experiences nervousness, fear, and anxiety after the walkout. They get an overwhelming urge to call the narcissist, and at this point, they are thriving off the chaotic feeling that the narcissist has created. The victim becomes addicted to his behaviors, and when he leaves, they miss him, and when the narcissist goes silent, it's absolute torment to the victim. They would rather that he was screaming in their face than saying nothing because at least he is showing some type of emotion and the victim knows where they stand. Despite the fact that the connection between the narcissist and his victim has been manufactured and manipulated, the victim has gotten to a point where they simply can't live without it. After an extended period of absence, the narcissist will turn up just before the victim can do anything stupid. He will reinforce the silent treatment knowing that his victim is just satisfied that she has access to him. The narcissist conditions his victims to keep lowering their standards so that he can get away with doing even more evil.

PSYCHOLOGICAL ABUSE IS ADDICTIVE

What does abuse look like to most people? If this question was put forward to the general public, most would speak of the evil physically abusive characters they see in films and on TV. They beat their partners, scream at them, and even kill them in fits of rage. Although abuse of this nature does take place, it does not provide an accurate representation of the abuse that people in the real-world experience. Therapist Shannon Thomas explains that psychological abuse is like a poison that slowly enters the veins through an IV drip.

It begins with an insult here and a back-handed comment there. The victim will typically brush these incidents off as random events because narcissists are experts at pretending that they are the perfect partner, and as stated, they will shower their partner with love and affection. As the mask begins to slip, the victim convinces herself that the narcissist's behavior is out of character and that they are the ones responsible for making their partner angry. People get trapped in these relationships because they believe that if only they try a little bit harder, they can win back their partner's affection. This cycle leads them to become addicted to the abuse in the same way that the addict becomes addicted to drugs.

A psychologically abusive relationship is like being on an emotional roller coaster. The victim is rewarded with kindness when they "behave" according to the narcissist's standards, but this is often inconsistent. This puts the body through trauma as a combination of cortisol (during punishment) and dopamine (during affection) is released. This causes the body to become biologically addicted to the treatment it is receiving. The victim is desperate for the connection she had with the narcissist at the beginning of the relationship, but what she fails to realize is that the connection was false. The nice side of the narcissist that was used to reel in the victim doesn't exist. After a while, this game of cat and mouse causes the body to become dependent on getting that approval. This hormonal rollercoaster puts a lot of stress on the body, and it manifests physically through conditions such as acne and chest pains, and in very severe cases, autoimmune disorders. The body will begin to shut down and experience arthritic type pains, migraines, chronic pains, and it will become difficult to fight infections.

Despite the stress that their bodies are being put through, victims stay in these relationships because they are unable to see clearly. They have become confused, disillusioned, and disorientated because of the intermittent love, control, and manipulation that the victim has been through. The narcissist has backed them into a corner of desperation and self-blame.

Due to traumatic bonding, if the victim does leave, they will eventually return, and others don't even make an attempt to leave. A relationship with a narcissist will always follow a pattern of idealization, devaluation, and discarding. Since narcissists depend on supply, if the victim becomes so broken that they are no longer capable of providing that supply, they abandon them permanently and move on to the next victim. Sometimes, this is the only way a victim will break free from her abuser, and it is at this point that the victim can come to terms with the fact that they have been in an abusive relationship. They will go through a grieving process in which they realize how damaged they have become and that nothing that happened to them was their fault. This is when healing can take place and the survivor is made aware that they were not targeted because they were weak, but because they had such a giving heart.

Here are signs that you or someone you know might be in a trauma bond:

- Your partner is always promising you things but never delivers
- Your partner does or says something to you around other people that disturbs them, but you brush it off or make excuses for his behavior
- You can't see any way out of the relationship, and you feel stuck
- You have constant arguments with your partner that never get resolved
- You are given the silent treatment or punished by your partner when you do or say something that he doesn't like

- You feel as if you can't detach yourself from your relationship even though deep down you know that something is wrong
- When you do leave the relationship, you feel as if you physically can't cope with being away from him
- You do everything you can to please your partner even though you know you are not getting the same treatment in return
- You desperately try to win his approval although it is obvious he is using you
- You continue to trust in him even though he is perpetually unreliable
- You desperately desire to be understood by your abusive partner even though it's clear he doesn't care
- You are loyal to your partner when he has betrayed you

HOW TO HEAL FROM TRAUMATIC BONDING

Once you get out of an abusive relationship with a narcissist, the healing process is essential for you to move forward in life. Here are some steps to help you.

See a Therapist: Therapy is essential to the healing process, as it will help you see things that you are unable to on your own. What you have been through will have severely damaged your mental health and will take some time to repair. A therapist will help you understand how you ended up in an abusive relationship. They will evaluate your childhood and explain how that contributed to you being attracted to such a person. They will also provide you with coping strategies to deal with the grieving process.

Allow Yourself to Grieve: At the end of the day, even though it's a good thing that you've gotten out of the relationship, you are still going to feel as if you have lost something. Regardless of whether you have been in the relationship for months or years, you are going to be upset that it has come to an end. You gave your heart and soul to a person who took advantage of you and abused you. The individual might not be worth mourning over, but the situation must be mourned so that you can move on with your life. You have experienced the death of a relationship, the death of the illusion that your relationship was under, and you have just come to the conclusion that you have been living a lie. According to grief expert Elisabeth Kubler-Ross, you will go through five stages of grief.

- **Denial:** At this stage, the world becomes overwhelming and meaningless. You can't understand why this had to happen to you, you are in a state of denial and shock. You feel numb inside and don't know how you are going to continue living. You will struggle to find reasons to live. However, shock and denial make it easier for you to cope with what has happened. Denial helps to process the feelings associated with grief. It is nature's way of only allowing in as much as we can handle. As time goes on, you will begin to accept that you have lost this person, and you will start asking yourself questions. This is when the healing process begins. You will start getting stronger, and you will start confronting your feelings instead of denying them.

- **Anger:** Anger is required for proper healing to take place, even though it will feel like it is never going to end. Accept your anger—the more you allow yourself to feel this emotion the less it will have control over you, and you will begin to heal. You will also experience

193

several other emotions during the stage of anger. They are different for each person, and you will become familiar with them as you go through them. Anger is limitless, and you will take it out on many people including family, friends, therapists, the person you ended the relationship with, and if you are religious, God. You will wonder whether God has abandoned you in all of this. Your anger is covering up the pain that you really feel—it is natural to feel abandoned and deserted. There is strength in anger. It serves as an anchor and provides temporary structure to the empty feeling of loss. In the beginning, grief feels as if you are lost at sea, in the middle of an ocean with nothing to hold onto. When you get angry, structure is formed, the anger allows you to connect to something, it builds a bridge over the endless sea that you feel that you are lost in, and now you have something to hold onto as you try and walk out this stage of grief. Although anger is not a nice feeling, it is better than the denial stage because at least you are feeling something. The anger that you feel is an indication of the intensity of the love that you felt for your partner.

The more you learn to love yourself, the angrier you will become. You will start to feel frustrated at the fact that you allowed someone to treat you in this way. When you start experiencing these emotions, take a drive somewhere, go to the beach or a secluded location and scream and cry, release every negative emotion from your system. Do this as many times as you need to. Never self-harm by cutting yourself, drinking, or taking drugs as a way of numbing the pain. Instead, face your emotions head on.

This is the only way you will prevent yourself from becoming a victim. If you want to beat this, harming yourself is not the way to do it.

- **Bargaining:** Bargaining comes in the form of *"what if…."* statements. No matter how destructive your relationship was, you will want it to go back to normal because you can't handle the feeling of that person no longer being in your life. You will want to rewind the hands of time, *"Could I have been a better girlfriend,"* *"What if I could cook better,"* *"What if I cleaned the house better?"* Guilt and bargaining go hand in hand, you will feel as if it was your fault that the relationship broke down and you will think about all the things that you could have done differently to make the relationship work. Since you know that you will never get your partner back, you may even start to bargain about the pain you are feeling, and begin to say things like, *"I would do anything not to feel like this anymore."* It is important to remember that these stages don't have a time limit—they can last for minutes, hours, weeks, or months. They are not stages that you step in and out of in chronological order, you will move back and forth between each of them. After the bargaining stage has ended, you will begin to focus your attention on the present, you will start to feel empty, and the feelings of grief will intensify.

- **Depression:** The feeling of depression will feel as if it will never end. You will feel as if you are stuck in the bottom of a black pit with no way out. Depression does not mean that you are suffering from mental illness, it is a normal stage of the grieving process. You are supposed to feel this way after losing someone that was a significant part of your life. You will feel intense sadness at this stage and wonder if you can continue living life alone. Even though you were in an abusive relationship, losing someone you love is depressing and this is an appropriate and normal response to what you are going through. Not to experience depression would be considered abnormal, and when it finally settles in your soul that you can't fix the relationship, that there is no going back, depression will take over you.

- **Acceptance:** This stage of the grieving process is often misinterpreted as being okay with what has happened, that you have gotten over it and you are moving on with your life. This is far from the truth. The majority of people will never be okay that they have lost someone important in their life and, in particular, that you spent the majority of those years being abused. It is going to take a while for you to get over this. The acceptance stage is about accepting that the relationship is over, you will never return to it, and that you are now living in a new normal. You must now try to live in a world where the person you loved is no longer a part of it. You can no longer pick up the phone and call him when you want, you can't turn up at his house, and he isn't going to be turning up at your house. That chapter of your life is now closed and it's time to move forward. Because of the abuse that you have endured, you may even feel like you are betraying your partner when you move on, especially when you learn how to be happy. When you have spent so much time being told that you don't deserve happiness, you start to believe it, which is part of the reason you stayed in the relationship in the first place. However, you must evolve, grow, and move onto greener pastures. As you start to invest in yourself and relationships with others, you will start living again. However, you will not be able to do so until you have given some time to the grieving process.

This idea is totally optional; however, it is worth mentioning because some abuse victims do report that it brings a sense of closure. You might want to take part in a burial ceremony in which you bury or burn all the belongings of your partner. Things like cards, letters, gifts, and clothes, you can either put them in a box and bury them, or you can burn them in a bonfire and say goodbye to them forever.

Live in the Moment: After an abusive relationship, people tend to focus on what could have been. Even though they are no longer in the relationship, due to the psychological damage that has taken place, they feel that if they had done things differently the relationship may have gone in a different direction. Survivors of psychological abuse fail to understand that what happened had nothing to do with them but everything to do with the abuser. Narcissists seek out people they can abuse, they know what they are doing is wrong, which is why they wear a mask at the beginning stages of the relationship. Therefore, instead of focusing on the past or the future, focus on the present, how you feel right now. Do you feel unloved, trapped, unworthy? Do you feel as if you compromised your morals and values to be in this relationship? Stop waiting and hoping and put your energy into what is taking place now and the effect it is having on you.

Process Your Emotions: When you have just left an abusive relationship, your emotions are going to be severely damaged, so it is important that you take some time out to process what you are feeling. You are going to miss your partner—you will feel alone, depressed, helpless, frustrated, and even angry. It is important that you don't suppress your emotions but recognize them as valid and accept them for what they are. A great way to release your emotions is to join a martial arts class. You will be able to release your pain on a punching bag instead of internalizing it.

Reconnect with Loved Ones: One of the main strategies of a narcissist is to isolate their victims. They will force you to cut ties with friends, family members, and loved ones because they don't want anyone else to influence you but them. If this is something you have experienced, make an effort to reconnect with the people you were once associated with. You will probably feel slightly embarrassed to do this since there may be people you haven't spoken to in months or even years. However, if they are level-headed people, when you explain your situation, they will understand. They will be able to encourage you and support you as you go through the healing process.

If you find this too difficult, look for opportunities to meet new people. A great way to do this is to join a domestic survivor's group. You will meet people exactly like you who have been in similar relationships. You will be able to relate to each other on a deeper level than those who have not experienced psychological abuse.

CHAPTER 7:

PROTECTION STRATEGY: HOW TO BREAK FREE FROM A NARCISSIST

You will experience several difficult phases when you are in a relationship with a narcissist. There are going to be times when you feel so abused, humiliated, and alone that all you want to do is give up. You will feel exhausted, worthless, and rejected. You will feel intense pain, but at the same time you will not want to face the reality of the situation, so you will convince yourself that things are okay just so that you can feel better. But in the long run, you will feel much worse as you begin to realize that you were only deceiving yourself. There are times when you will feel as if you are in a prison and there is no escape. This process is going to be challenging, but you must start somewhere. Start by training yourself to become immune to their egocentrism. Here are some steps to do this.

- Be determined and independent, live your life the way you want to.
- Don't allow discussions and arguments to drain your emotions and energy.

- Stop giving the person compliments, attention, and praise—these things are what fuel the narcissist.
- Keep your conversations with the person short. Narcissists enjoy being at the center of attention, and by engaging with them, you are feeding them energy.
- Do not stoop to the same level as the narcissist. As much as they are annoying you and you want to give them a taste of their own medicine, this is not a good idea. The narcissist will enjoy going back and forth with you, and in the end, you will lose. Remember, the narcissist is an experienced player, you are not.

After a while, the narcissist in your life will get fed up with you. They only stick around when they have something to gain, and since you are no longer providing them with narcissistic supply because their behavior and comments don't have an effect on you, they will look elsewhere. Once they find another victim, just know that your name will be dragged through the dirt. They will tell their new partner how terrible you were and how badly you treated them to make their next victim feel sorry for them.

Once they have left, you will go through a grieving period in which you will start to feel pity for the narcissist. You will convince yourself that they are only like this because they are deeply depressed. There is no need to feel this way, everything that the narcissist says or does is calculated and well thought out. They do not act on impulse or from a place of despair. They know exactly what they are doing. The narcissist only starts feeling depressed when they have run out of supply; therefore, they will go out looking for new stimuli (alcohol, drugs, the opposite sex, shopping). Once they get their supply, they are back to their normal selves again. Instead of spending time feeling sorry for yourself, engage in the following to get over this feeling of guilt that you are experiencing.

- Eat well and exercise, take care of your physical body.
- Go for a walk and meet up with people who will make you feel better.
- Talk to people you trust to get it out of your system.
- Cry and shout for as long as you need to.
- Relax by taking a long bath or shower.
- Go to the movies or rent a film—this will take your mind off what is going on in your own life.
- Start journaling—this will help you to get in touch with your emotions and release the ones that are of no benefit to you.
- Buy yourself something nice.
- Become a volunteer—this will show you that there are more important people to take care of than your narcissistic partner.
- Take part in alternative therapies such as Eye Movement Desensitization and Reprocessing (EMDR) or Emotional Freedom Technique (EFT). They are effective therapies that assist in releasing and overcoming painful emotions.
- Surround yourself with positive people who will give you hope that there is light at the end of the tunnel.
- Get rid of anything in your house that reminds you of your partner.
- If your partner was controlling and only allowed you to wear the clothes that they liked, give those clothes to charity and start wearing clothes that you like.
- The attention that you once gave to your narcissistic partner should now be given to yourself.

Now that you know you are dealing with a narcissist, your next step is to get as far away from them as possible. This is the hard part! As you have read, extreme narcissists have no empathy whatsoever. They don't take responsibility for their actions and make everyone around them feel terrible within a couple of weeks of being in their presence. It is highly unlikely that they are even remotely aware of how they are behaving, and it is even more unlikely that they are going to take a good look in the mirror and decide that they need to change.

Since you are a normal person who has feelings and genuinely cares for people, you are going to be tempted to want to help the narcissist to see the error of their ways, but this is not a good idea. It will backfire on you—their defenses will go up and they may even manage to convince you that you are the one with the problem. With an extreme narcissist, it is highly unlikely that you are going to get a fair deal, and by keeping them in your life, you are going to stay miserable.

You will need to make a decision, and you will need to make it quickly. No relationship is easy to cut off, but the easiest (and I use the word "easiest" lightly) are going to be romantic partners, colleagues, friends, and in some cases, family members. In most cases, you are not legally bound to remain in a relationship with these people. For example, you don't have joint ownership of a property, you don't own a business together, there is no dependent involved, or there is no will administration taking place. When you are free from these circumstances, escaping from such a relationship is viable. Although it is going to be a difficult decision because you might genuinely care for the person, nobody deserves to stay in a relationship that is causing them emotional damage. Breaking all contact means closing every window, door, and mailbox. Block them on all social media platforms and don't allow them to contact you by email, text, or chat. If any gap is left open, they will do everything in their power to get back in your good books. Don't read old text messages or listen to voicemails. Hearing them begging and pleading may make you feel sorry for them so that you fall into the trap they have laid for you. After you cut them off, everything they are going to say to you will come from a place of anger and manipulation, and this is not conducive to the healing process.

Although you will never completely forget about this person, you really don't want to keep them at the forefront of your memory. Therefore, it's a good idea to ask friends and family not to speak about the person or ask you if you have heard from them. You should also ask them not to provide any information about you. The dangerous thing about narcissists is that they are so charming, everyone loves them. There is a high possibility that your friends and family members won't understand why you have decided to end the relationship. More often than not, he will be in the good books of your friends and family, and he will use this as a way to get in contact with you again. He will turn up at your parents' house crying, saying he doesn't understand why you have done this to him, *"Please give me her number, I just want to talk, I just want to understand what I have done wrong, so I can fix it."* Your loved ones will need to be very stern and let him know in no uncertain terms that they will not be providing any contact information.

In the beginning stages of the breakup, it is essential that you don't spend too much time alone. First, you are going to feel lonely. You were probably in a relationship with this individual for quite some time and now you are on your own. Second, too much alone time will get you thinking, and you will start to ask yourself if you have really done the right thing. It is very important during this time to be as distracted as possible so that you don't go back.

Don't waste any time blaming yourself thinking you could have done something to change the situation. Unfortunately, this way of thinking is not new to you. Victims of narcissist abuse are made to feel that everything that is happening to them is their fault. They spend a lot of time and energy trying to work out what they could do better or what they shouldn't have done to cause this. Please understand that it is impossible to change a narcissist—you don't have the power to do so. They can only change themselves. The only person you have the power to change is yourself, and this is what you should focus your attention on. Your thought process should be as follows: *"You were once in a terrible and unhealthy relationship; it is over and now you must focus on healing yourself."*

Another emotion you will have to deal with is the pain of knowing that your ex-partner was never really in love with you. Love is not evil—it does not cause pain and distress. This realization is very difficult to cope with, and it will make you feel unlovable. You will start to question whether you deserved to be treated in this way. As much as it hurts, thinking like this is a waste of time and energy. You have to look at the facts, regardless of a person's definition of love or whether they are capable of showing love or not, your standards dictate that you should never have been treated in this way. You will never find true love with someone with a personality disorder—they are incapable of loving anyone, not even themselves.

When you catch yourself thinking about whether your partner loved you, change your thought process and begin to tell yourself that you are worthy of love, you are valuable and there are people who will love you unconditionally, people who will not exploit you mentally and emotionally.

EDUCATE YOURSELF ABOUT MENTAL ILLNESS

This book has only just scratched the surface about narcissistic personality disorder. The more you know about the condition, the easier it will be for you not to end up in a similar relationship. Read books, search the internet, go to seminars, do whatever you need to do to find out as much about this disorder as possible.

The above is the only way you can become completely detached from the individual. However, if this is too extreme for you and you feel that you need to make a slow exit, there are other options which we will look at in the next chapter.

CHAPTER 8:

PROTECTION STRATEGY: HOW TO SLOWLY DETACH YOURSELF FROM A NARCISSIST

t is very difficult to break up with a narcissistic partner. They have the ability to make you fall so deeply in love with them that it feels as if you are cutting out a part of your heart when you leave them. They will also use every trick they know to manipulate you into coming back. Therefore; sometimes, the best way to get out of a relationship with a narcissist is to do so slowly.

TAKE A BREAK

You can choose to manage the situation the best way you can, or you can step back and take a break from the individual. Taking a break can help you analyze the relationship from a distance and help you gain some clarity. If you are in a physically abusive relationship, taking a break is not an option, you need to cut ties with that person permanently.

Who you choose to spend your time with is important, not only because you deserve to be treated with dignity and respect, but because it is easy to be influenced by those around you. Yale University Professor Nicholas Christakis refers to this as "the ripple effect." What he means by this is that the characteristics of a person, whether good or bad, will ripple through the people they are surrounded by. Whatever you are exposed to will affect your personal development and if it is negative, expect your spirit to be infiltrated with all manner of evil. If the people you associate with are positive, you have gained something good in life.

Tell your partner that you need some space, that you are going to stay with a friend or a family member. I am warning you that he is not going to be very happy with this decision and he will attempt to do everything to stop you from leaving. Deep down, he will know you are thinking about leaving, and narcissists don't like getting dumped. However, don't fall for any of his tactics. Take a break and enjoy life without him for a while. When you make the decision to voluntarily leave, you will be able to see things differently because the shoe is on the other foot. It's not him walking out on you and leaving you in an emotional mess, you have the power now. Turn off your phone and don't allow him to contact you, it will give you the opportunity to discover what it feels like not to get abused.

DON'T GET TOO CLOSE

If you have no choice but to keep a narcissist in your life, you will need to learn the art of feeding them with a long-handled spoon. Keeping them at a distance is your safest option, but you will need to be clever about it. Narcissists are strange people—it is when you get too close to them that they begin to undervalue you. However, when you have set boundaries that you won't allow them to cross, they gain respect for you. Additionally, keeping your distance will ensure that what you say is never misinterpreted as competition or a threat to the narcissist, as they have a tendency to twist people's words and read too much into what a person is saying when they get too close to them.

Stop Giving Him Narcissistic Supply

If you find it too difficult to break up with a narcissist, make them break up with you. A narcissist will stay in a relationship when they are benefitting from it. However, as soon as the supply is cut off, they move on to the next. Their dependence on supply is their weakness, and when you are the one giving it to them, the power is in your hands. Here are two of the most powerful ways you can cut off narcissistic supply.

Show No Emotion

The narcissist feeds off your emotions—he loves to see you get angry, sad, and frustrated when he launches an attack. The goal is to show absolutely no emotion whatsoever so that it becomes glaringly obvious that he no longer has any control over you. Stop getting angry when he provokes you, don't get sad when he gives you the silent treatment, and don't react to his shaming and blaming tactics. Please understand that the narcissist has the emotional intelligence of a five-year-old, so refuse to take his behavior personally. Five-year-olds have no clue what they are doing, and to some extent, even though the narcissist is very calculating and manipulative, they have no idea of what they are doing.

See Them as Objects of Study

The more you understand the behavior of a narcissist, the easier it will be to outsmart them. Look at him as a social experiment, examine him and watch him as if you are zoologist observing a lion from a safe distance. Watch him without engaging with him. When you become aware of the complexities of a narcissist, you will no longer want to feed the monster when you know how dangerous this can be.

CHAPTER 9:

PROTECTION STRATEGY: HOW TO CREATE BOUNDARIES WITH A NARCISSIST

I n situations where you can't completely break contact with a narcissist, you can protect yourself by establishing boundaries and sticking to them. As you may well know, narcissists don't have boundaries and neither do they like it when other people put limits on their intrusions. However, if you stick to them, there is not much they can do about it but accept them. Here are some tips on how to set boundaries with narcissists.

KNOW YOUR LIMITS

Narcissists can be very rude and aggressive. They will call you names and bully you, especially if you don't jump when they tell you to. If you are not willing to tolerate name-calling, bullying, and rudeness, tell them. For example, if you are in the middle of a conversation and they start acting up, say: *"Listen if you keep acting the way you are, I will put an end to this conversation until you are capable of showing me some respect."* You don't need to give an explanation or a reason. If they choose not to take you seriously and they continue, say: *"As I mentioned, your rudeness is unaccept-able, and I am not willing to talk to you when you act like this, good-bye."* Either hang up the phone or walk out of the room. Don't engage in any further conversation with them and don't allow them to respond. The more decisively and quickly you act the easier it will be to disarm the narcissist.

The narcissist is likely to continue with their abuse. They may try to call you or follow you and attempt to convince you that you are being unfair or that you are going over the top. They will try a number of different approaches to see if they can confuse, intimidate, or get you to feel guilty about your decision.

While their begging and the pressure they are putting you under is uncomfortable, your boundaries are not up for negotiation. Sticking to your decision will lead you to feel stronger, less overwhelmed, safer, and calmer.

HAVE A PLAN OF ESCAPE

You don't need permission to leave an unhealthy interaction with another person. There are a variety of techniques you can use to get out of a conversation. For example, you can take a quick look at your watch and say, *"Oh my goodness, is that the time, I need to leave."* Then walk out.

What you are saying you are late for is irrelevant. With a nar-cissist, every minute you allow them to abuse you is one more minute you allow them to get into your head.

Or you can glance at your phone and say, *"I'm really sorry, but I've got an important call I need to take."* You can do this whether your phone is ringing or not.

Or, since you already know the narcissist's character, set an alarm on your phone in advance and once the alarm goes off, excuse yourself.

YOU DECIDE WHAT YOU WANT TO TALK ABOUT

Politicians are good at doing this. When they are being in-
terviewed, you rarely hear them answering the question they
were asked. They talk about what they want to talk about. In
the same way, when a narcissist asks you a question that you
are not comfortable with, change the subject. If they ask you
what's going on in your relationship or how you are handling
your finances, and they have a bad habit of criticizing you
for the way you spend your money or conduct yourself in
a relationship, why put yourself through that again? Instead,
change the tide of the conversation and start talking about
something you know the narcissist loves discussing. For example, you could ask them how they learned to manage their
money so well, and if they have found the secrets to the perfect
relationship. Although they are now going to spend your time
talking about themselves, at least you are no longer the focus
of the conversation.

DON'T GIVE TOO MUCH INFORMATION

Limit the amount of private information you share with a narcissist. The less they know about you, the less ammunition they
have to use against you. If they have something negative to say
about what you are doing say, *"I am confident in the decisions I have
made."* Or, *"I have taken note of your opinion."*

NAME WHAT THEY ARE DOING

Narcissists are always trying to see how much they can get away
with and will push the limits in a relationship. They want to be
the center of attention at all times. One way to put a stop to this
is to say, *"I notice that any time I start talking about myself you cut*

me off to talk about you." Or, *"That sounded like you were trying to put me down."* You don't need to say anything else after that, just state the facts and leave it alone. What they say afterward is irrelevant. You have put your mark on the conversation by letting them know that you know what they are up to.

TAKE THE FOCUS OFF THEM

Narcissists live for attention—they love being praised, complimented, and admired. When you engage in conversation with them, they make sure they are the main focus. What you are feeling, experiencing, or going through is irrelevant to them. Whatever they believe, say, or need at that moment is their main priority, and they expect you to agree with them. To avoid being swept into the tide, perform a mental check every so often when you are communicating with a narcissist. Take note of what you are thinking, feeling, and wanting. If you find it too difficult to do this in the moment, when you have left the conversation, go over it and remember how you were thinking and feeling at the time. When you are aware of what is going on, you reduce the power of the narcissist to suffocate you with their agenda. If you ever attend a self-help group, you will hear the term *"gray rock"* when they are referring to narcissists. This means toning down how much you allow yourself to care about a narcissist. For that period of time you are with them, become as impenetrable as a rock. This is a way of disassociating yourself in an emotionally unsafe environment. The gray rock approach is a reminder that you are not going to give them your energy, neither are you going to fully engage with them, you reserve this type of normal behavior for safe people. Reacting emotionally or showing vulnerability around a narcissist gives them the green light to continue to abuse you even more.

Narcissists enjoy getting an emotional reaction out of people; in their perverted mind, it lets them know that they exist. By showing that they have an effect on you, you encourage their unhealthy intrusions and behaviors. Of course, narcissists are experts at getting people to react to their foolishness, so there are going to be times when you slip up no matter how hard you try not to. However, when you catch yourself, change the subject or excuse yourself.

REALIZE THAT YOU WILL HAVE TO KEEP SETTING BOUNDARIES WITH A NARCISSIST

In the majority of cases, when you are dealing with normal people, you can set boundaries once, and they will abide by them and you won't have to set them again. This is not the case with narcissists. They will continuously push against the boundaries you set in an attempt to wear you down. Therefore, if you want to keep those boundaries, you will need to keep re-establishing them.

DON'T BE TOO HARD ON YOURSELF

If you fail to set healthy boundaries or you slip up every once in a while, don't be too hard on yourself. Narcissists are very skilled individuals, and in most cases, this is someone you have been dealing with for years and you have only just decided to put your foot down. In such instances, you will have years of vulnerability to deal with, and that is a lot to get over. Allow yourself room for error, and when you realize you have messed up, ask yourself what you will do differently next time.

FOCUS ON IMPROVING YOURSELF

Narcissists care about appearance and image, so whoever they are with, they expect them to act in a way that validates them, this is typically at your expense. You have to decide who you are going to be around a narcissist, ask yourself:

- Do I want to feel confident and strong? Or overwhelmed and small?
- What am I standing for right now?
- How can I give myself the utmost respect in this situation?

The answers you provide will give you some important insight into the person you want to be at that moment.

REMEMBER WHO YOU ARE DEALING WITH

Narcissists are extremely needy, and underneath their fake exterior, they feel inferior and empty. The wall of confidence they have built around themselves is to hide how they really feel from the rest of the world. When you know the truth about a narcissist, it allows you to see them for who they really are as opposed to the bully who thinks they know everything and has the power to reduce you to a whimpering five-year-old. Remind yourself that the narcissist has a hard life, and the constant need for approval must be extremely draining. In no way am I suggesting that their issues justify their controlling and abusive behavior, but what it does do is remind you not to take what they do personally and, to a certain extent, have compassion on them.

ENFORCE THE CONSEQUENCES

If the narcissist is not willing to respect your boundaries, you will need to enforce consequences. This is the only way you will let them know that you are serious. Before you meet up with a narcissist, decide what the consequences are going to be if your boundaries are ignored or violated. What you don't want to happen is that you try to work out what the consequences are going to be in the middle of a situation. Once you have told the narcissist what the consequences are going to be, enforce them immediately, don't give any explanation, don't waste time, just do it. If not, you will reap the consequences of not enforcing them, which is playing the narcissist's game.

When you start setting boundaries, narcissists will up their attack. They may start spreading rumors and gossip about you or threaten to disown you. This is the risk you take when choosing to have a narcissist in your life. You will also need to think about these potential consequences that your boundaries could lead to. It may need to be the case that you choose your battles wisely instead of getting them so angry that they have a personal vendetta against you.

CHAPTER 10:

PROTECTION STRATEGY: HOW TO STOP AN ARGUMENT WITH A NARCISSIST

O bject constancy is when a person finds it difficult to have positive and negative feelings at the same time. For example, when a narcissist is ready to have a fight, they can be extremely vicious because all they understand at the time are their feelings of anger and resentment. This can lead to an argument about something seemingly insignificant turning into something fierce. If the narcissist is violent, the smallest issue can cause them to strike their partner or start throwing things.

Depending on their sub-type, narcissists have the tendency to be very fragile. They get offended easily and will accuse their partner of being selfish or disrespectful if they dare to put their needs first. In their eyes, the world revolves around them so if their partner focuses on anything else, they see it as a direct insult. Psychologists have yet to work out whether this behavior is conscious or not, and if they actually mean to cause the harm they do when they fly into a rage.

EXPECT A SEVERE ALTERCATION

Fighting with a narcissist is not like anything you will ever experience. Because of their hypersensitive nature and lack of empathy, they are wired to be abusive; therefore, it is normal for them to have zero understanding for someone else's needs and take offense at the slightest misunderstanding. Narcissistic rage has levels—they might give their partner the silent treatment for hours or have a screaming match in which they verbally abuse their partner with hurtful names. Or they will just walk out and find someone else to sleep with in the coldest and calculating manner. If you find yourself in this position with a narcissist, there are some strategies you can implement to deescalate the situation.

DON'T GET INTO AN ARGUMENT ABOUT RIGHT OR WRONG

You are wasting your time if you think you are ever going to win an argument with a narcissist; even if they are in the wrong, they are never going to admit it. They will want you to take responsibility for every negative emotion you are feeling because they are totally dependent on keeping up the image that they are perfect and can do nothing wrong.

TRY TO EMPATHIZE WITH HOW THEY ARE FEELING

Most people who are in a relationship with a narcissist have a lot of empathy anyway. However, even the most empathetic person finds it difficult to have empathy for someone who is bashing them with insults. If you find that you have been backed into a corner, one way to calm a narcissist down is to say something like, *"What I did must have been very hurtful for you, I can understand why you are so angry."* In this way, you are letting them know that you are taking responsibility for your actions, even though you know you have done nothing wrong.

You Are in This Together

Do not use language such as *"you"* or *"I,"* instead say *"we,"* in this way, you are indirectly saying that you are also to blame for what is taking place. The narcissist is going to be extremely angry because you had the audacity to defend yourself, so to prevent the argument from escalating, remind them that you are in this together.

Ask about Something They are Interested in

Narcissists love to talk about themselves or to display how much they know about a certain subject. So, in the same way you would distract a baby with a toy, you can distract the narcissist with a new conversation to steer the conversation out of an argument. This probably won't work in the middle of a screaming row; it is more effective if you do it before the argument has escalated or after the flames have died down.

Another strategy is to ask the narcissist for advice. They take pride in the fact that they have reduced you to a dependent child who can't do anything unless they sanction it. It will make the narcissist feel that they are the only person you can go to and it will make them feel superior.

Don't Take the Bait

Since the narcissist believes you have severely hurt them, they will want to get revenge on you. To do so, they will throw everything they think you've ever done to them back in your face, and on top of that, remind you of how selfish you are being now. Their main aim is to get you to react emotionally, so your best response is to ignore the comments. By responding, you will simply encourage another argument, which is what you are trying to avoid.

Don't Expect an Apology

A narcissist will never admit they are in the wrong, so don't even ask for an apology. The most important thing is that you know that you didn't do anything to deserve what just took place. Trying to get the narcissist to see things from your point of view is a waste of time and energy. It is also important that you don't ask them to process what just happened. They will feel very uncomfortable reminding themselves that they started an argument over something so trivial, so the best thing to do is to leave it alone.

CHAPTER 11:

PROTECTION STRATEGY: PRACTICE GIVING BALANCED LOVE

The narcissist feeds off their victim's fear, and the victim feels that in order to gain the narcissist's approval, to gain their love and to feel worthy, they must never disappoint the narcissist. The narcissist takes full advantage of their victim's needs and desire to be loved, wanted, seen as loving, kind, nice, and unselfish by them. The narcissists view these traits as a sign of inferiority and weakness and will take every opportunity to disrupt their partner's feelings of security and self-worth and replace them with self-blame, self-doubt, and fear.

To overcome this, the victim must take responsibility for their own healing and choose to put themselves first. They must understand that it's impossible to put a stop to what the narcissist is doing if they don't work to change themselves from within. This is essential because, in reality, the way you treat yourself is the only thing that human beings have complete and total control over. To start, here are some strategies that the victim can implement.

- Create an emotional detachment from the need to rescue the narcissist from their self-sabotaging behaviors.
- Refuse to allow the narcissist to treat you like a punching bag.
- Refuse to depend on the narcissist for safety, feelings of value, and self-worth.
- Realize that the narcissist will never care for you unless they first relinquish their false sense of reality.
- Understand that trying to get validation from a narcissist is like attempting to get blood out of a stone.

The right actions will begin to follow once you reach this place; however, it is not going to be easy, especially if you have been in the relationship for several years. Old ingrained habits will keep coming up, and you will need to work to shut them down. The victim must learn to completely emotionally detach themselves from the narcissist but do so in a loving way. There is no need to stoop to the same level as the narcissist during this process, which will feed into what they want. Remember, the narcissist wants to get a rise out of you, so if you get angry and start hurling insults at them, they have won. The narcissist will enjoy the fact that you are giving them an excuse to continue arguing with you.

To detach yourself means that you have shifted your focus from taking care of the needs, wants, and desires of the narcissist onto yourself. Instead of trying to rescue them, you are now rescuing yourself. You are rescuing your self-respect and sanity and cultivating the self-acceptance and compassion that will free yourself from toxic behavioral patterns.

It is essential to understand that you have no power to change the narcissist. Unless they decide that the way they are living is not benefiting them, they will never change. Until this happens, you will never be in a safe place with a narcissist, so don't listen to what they have to say. Narcissists can talk a good game, but their actions will determine whether they are serious or not.

CHAPTER 12:

PROTECTION STRATEGY: CUT ALL PSYCHIC CORDS

I f you are not sure what a psychic cord is (also known as an etheric cord), let me explain. Have you ever gotten so deeply involved in a conversation with someone that long after the discussion has ended, you are still emotionally involved in the other person's issues? A lot of empaths experience this due to the sensitive nature of their spirit. It feels as if you are still having the conversation because it is continuously playing in your head. This is how the majority of people feel the effects of a psychic cord.

Psychic cords connect you to loved ones including friends, family, romantic partners, and pets. They assist in transmitting the exchange of feelings, thoughts, and energy. When the connection is healthy, the cord will transmit telepathic information and love between two people and intensify the connection between them both. However, when you are in a relationship with a narcissist who abuses you, this connection is not healthy. In your case, it is important that the cord is severed.

UNHEALTHY PSYCHIC CORDS – THE NEGATIVE EFFECTS

Unhealthy psychic cords drain your energy. They will challenge your mental health and make you feel physically sick. Psychic cords are typically created with people that you have empathetic feelings towards. It is common for healers to experience this with their clients. When a mother looks after her sick child, she transmits some of her energy to assist in the healing process. Caregivers, nurses, and teachers have a tendency to experience unhealthy psychic cords. Any type of co-dependent relationship will be bound by unhealthy psychic cords. People will cut these cords in an effort to release themselves from negative energy that no longer benefits them.

Ethers are like auras—they help to maintain the physical body and can also assist in connecting with spiritual entities that are on a higher plane. If you were to describe a psychic cord physically, it is compared to an umbilical cord. In a loving and healthy relationship, this cord extends through the heart chakra and good energy is exchanged back and forth. In an unbalanced or unhealthy relationship, this cord extends through the naval area or the solar plexus where energy is leached between two people. Those who make you feel sympathy or pity and you are constantly concerned for them may have a cord attached to you and you are not aware of it. This can prevent good things from taking place in your life because you are continuously caught up in their negative energy. It is important that you are aware of how someone else's negative energy can affect your life. In the case of an unhealthy relationship in which you have been abused, it is essential that the cord is severed and never reconnected.

How to Cut Psychic Cords

Although you have just been through months or possibly years of abuse, it is essential that the psychic cord you have with your ex-partner is cut with love. When you dissolve the connection, you are sending it back to the Creator or whatever it is that you believe in has divine power over you. Release any fears or judgments you may have about having a psychic cord with such an abusive person and about any way that you may have participated. Once the cord has been cut, your vitality and energy will be restored immediately. You will clear your emotions and free your mind so that you can focus on moving forward with your life. The results are typically subtle, but sometimes they can have a massively positive effect on you. When unhealthy psychic cords are released, you open the door to new and unlimited opportunities in your life. Here are a few techniques you can use to cut unhealthy psychic cords.

- Stand with your arms stretched out in front of you and then cross your arms over each other as if you are making a large X shape.
- Starting with your hands positioned at your groin area (root chakra), slightly move one hand a couple of inches up from the body. Keep raising your arm slowly until it is raised over the top of your head.
- Call upon the archangel Michael to sever the psychic cord in the purest and highest of ways.
- Meditate on cutting the cord and ask that any lessons learned from the experience are revealed to you. Send forgiveness to your ex-partner, visualize that the cords have severed their purpose and have been turned back into love.

Spend some time in gratitude that you have severed these cords, do some deep breathing exercises, and start thinking about how you can move forward in life.

CHAPTER 13:

PROTECTION STRATEGY: RECLAIM YOUR LIFE

Emotional abuse is deeply damaging, and without going through the healing process, you make yourself even more vulnerable to entering into the same type of relationship. You have been violated psychologically, and you will experience anxiety, depression, dissociation, feelings of low self-esteem, low self-worth, nightmares, and flashbacks. As mentioned in chapter 6, it is essential that you seek counseling to assist you in the healing process; however, there are strategies you can implement in your daily life that will help you to move forward.

YOGA

The effects of trauma live in the body, yoga is a combination of physical activity and mindfulness that help to establish and restore balance. Research has proven that yoga alleviates anxiety and depression, it improves symptoms of post-traumatic stress disorder in victims of domestic violence, boosts self-esteem, and improves body image. Yoga involves a series of powerful movements that compensate for the feelings of powerlessness that victims of abuse are left with.

Dr. Bessel Van der Kolk has spent years studying the benefits of yoga, and he believes that it allows traumatized victims to take back ownership of their bodies. Trauma robs abuse victims of a sense of safety, and yoga helps them reconnect through the use of bodily sensations.

MEDITATION

Trauma disrupts the area in the brain responsible for memory, learning, emotion regulation, and planning. Research has found that meditation benefits the same areas of the brain that are affected by trauma such as the hippocampus, the amygdala, and the prefrontal cortex. Meditation gives abuse victims their psyche back. It heals the brain and allows them to respond to life from a place of empowerment instead of a place of trauma.

Daily meditation practice strengthens the neural pathways in the brain and boosts grey matter density in areas of the brain related to the fight or flight response and emotion regulation. Meditation also allows you to become aware of your need to make contact with your abuser. When victims are not aware of this, they make impulse decisions which usually leads to them returning to the relationship. It also makes you more aware of your emotions in general.

ANCHOR YOURSELF

In general, emotional abuse survivors have been gaslighted into believing that they were imagining the abuse they were experiencing. It is essential that you start anchoring yourself into the reality of the fact that you were abused, but you are no longer in that abusive situation. It is common for abuse victims to idealize the relationship they were in and spend time thinking about what could have been if only they were capable of pleasing their partner. Connecting to reality also helps when struggling with mixed emotions towards your abuser. As mentioned, one of the strategies of the narcissist is to show affection and withdraw it, and it is the affectionate side of the narcissist that victims are drawn to. The narcissist seeks to erode the reality of their victim, but once you are reconnected with your reality, you are able to see your abuser for who he truly is.

Survivors are extremely vulnerable when they get out of an abusive relationship; their abusers will revert back to displaying their loving and affectionate side to manipulate them into coming back. This is why it is essential that you block phone calls and texts and any other form of contact so that he has no way of getting into your head. This allows you to connect to what really happened to you instead of allowing him to convince you that your version of events is incorrect.

To start the anchoring process, make a list of ten of the most abusive incidents that took place during your relationship. When you get tempted to reconnect with your abuser, read this list and remind yourself of how evil he was to you, how he degraded you and made you feel less than human. You can also write down statements about how he made you feel such as: *"My abuser made me feel that I wasn't worth anything." "My abuser made me feel depressed," "My abuser made me feel that I was stupid." "My abuser made me feel as if I was getting what I deserved and that no one could ever love me the way he did."* Remind yourself of these feelings any time you are tempted to pick up the phone and call him or go to his house and see him. Ask yourself whether it feels good for someone to make you believe this about yourself. The more you remember the negative feelings associated with the relationship, the easier it will be to stay away.

WORK WITH YOUR INNER CHILD, SELF-SOOTHING

You didn't just happen to fall into an abusive relationship, there are some deep-rooted issues within you that have led you to this point in your life, and they typically stem from childhood. Through therapy, you will discover that there were some fundamental needs that were not met during childhood. In attempting to fill that void, you settled for an abusive relationship. Once you discover what that void is, it is essential that you learn what is required to fill it, so that you do not leave yourself vulnerable to enter into another abusive relationship. During the healing process, you will need to be extremely compassionate with yourself because of what you went through as a child, and the abuse you have endured is not your fault. Abuse has the power to open up old wounds that were never healed. The belief system that you have never felt good enough has always been a part of your psyche. Your abusive partner simply confirmed how you have always felt. When you are healing, it is essential that you change the narrative that is taking place in your mind, which is important in general, but even more so when you are recovering from abuse. Self-compassion can be the most powerful form of compassion, so it is important that you are gentle with yourself during this time.

When you start feeling these negative emotions, comfort yourself as if you were speaking to a child who is being bullied in the playground. Tell yourself that you are the opposite of everything the negative self-chatter is trying to speak to your mind. You can say things such as, *"I am worthy of love," "I am special," "I deserve great things to happen in my life."* Over time, you will learn to stop blaming yourself and begin to overcome the toxic shame you have been subjected to. When you are judging yourself for what happened, you are more likely to indulge in self-sabotaging behaviors. But you can erase this by showing yourself compassion and reminding yourself that you are worthy of being kind and caring for yourself.

EXERCISE

Whether it's going for long intensive walks, going for a jog, joining a dance class, or joining the gym, incorporating exercise into your daily routine will really help during the healing process. If you don't have any motivation, don't try and do too much at once; for example, you can start off by going for a ten-minute walk and then increase it as time goes on. Exercise lowers cortisol levels and releases endorphins, which helps to replace the biochemical addiction you developed with your abuser with something that will benefit you. This addiction was formed through chemicals such as cortisol, dopamine, serotonin, and adrenaline which strengthen the bond with your abuser and form the cycle of highs and lows. Exercise allows you to build a wall of strength and resilience after leaving an abuser. It also helps to eliminate a lot of the physical problems associated with the abuse such as weight gain, sleep problems, premature aging, and a depleted immune system.

PUT UNHEALTHY COPING STRATEGIES TO BED

You did everything possible to try to keep your narcissistic partner happy and to keep him from flying into a fit of rage. Your days were spent walking on eggshells—you learned how to be silent and submissive, to question your every move, and to start all your conversations with the words, *"I'm sorry."* You learned how to dodge bullets and avoid landmines and act as if parts of your dreams, desires, and needs didn't exist. You learned how to devalue yourself and accept treatment from another human being that was totally unacceptable. The mental anguish you had to go through just to experience even a little bit of peace and keep yourself, and maybe your children, safe from harm was astounding. All these terrible things you had to learn were not only unhealthy, but in a normal relationship, they are not skills that will serve you well; therefore, you must learn new and normal habits that will benefit you in a healthy relationship. Unlearning old habits involves a system of self-monitoring; there are two types, qualitative and quantitative.

- Qualitative Monitoring: This involves being attentive to the old habits that you are engaging in—what do they look like and how do they make you feel?

- Quantitative Monitoring: This involves counting the old habits that don't serve you to monitor how many times you are engaging in them throughout the day.

Although both types of self-monitoring are effective, quantitative monitoring is most beneficial because for the first time you can accurately measure how you are behaving and the triggers that cause these bad habits to resurface. Previously, you may have had a slight idea of how bad your problem was, but now you can actually see it as well as have something to measure your progress by.

It is important that you establish a system for the self-monitoring process. It should include what you are monitoring, how you are going to record your observations, and how often the monitoring process will take place. For example, one of the most common coping strategies for women in an abusive relationship is normalizing the abuse. They do this by convincing themselves that they deserve the treatment, or even by telling themselves that other women go through this too, so it must just be what men do. It is impossible to monitor every single one of your thoughts, sometimes you are not consciously aware that you are thinking like this. However, there are going to be times when you catch yourself, and it is at this point that you should record the information. There doesn't need to be anything complicated about this process, simply carry a notebook with you and jot down the information. If you realize that something triggered you to start thinking this way, write that down too. Write down the date, the time, the thought, what triggered you, and how you felt when you started to think this way.

Learn to Love Yourself

This might sound cliché, but it is essential if you are going to move on with your life and eventually get into a healthy relationship. When you love yourself, you know who you are and what you stand for. It is impossible for anyone to come along and try to convince you that you are anything less than the best! When you develop a certain level of confidence and self-worth, nothing can shake you. Here are some tips on how to love yourself after an abusive relationship.

- **Get in Shape:** When you look good, you feel good! We have already discussed the benefits of exercise, so looking good is simply an added bonus. Make a decision not only to improve your health but to transform your body. Whatever your ideal weight and shape are, aim for that.

- **Change Your Wardrobe:** Once you have achieved your ideal body shape, treat yourself to some new clothes. You don't need to break the bank but buy some signature pieces that are really going to make you feel good about yourself.

- **Have Fun Alone:** Take one day out of the week and do something that you enjoy. A lot of abuse victims have difficulty being alone, which is why they are such easy prey for abusers. Spending time alone will teach you how to enjoy your own company. Things you could do might include, going to the movies, out to dinner, or finding a new hobby.

- **Try Something New:** Do things that you wouldn't normally do. Try something new and crazy like sky-diving or bungee jumping. That's a bit extreme, but you know yourself better than anyone else, so you can choose something that you know will add an element of surprise to your life.

- **Go on Vacation:** Even if you don't make it a regular thing, take a vacation somewhere. Go to a country that's completely out of your comfort zone. If you are not brave enough to go alone, invite a friend. Experience a different culture, new food, different activities, and have fun.

- **Journal:** Journaling is a good way to release any negative emotions you are feeling. It is also a good way of tracking your progress. Wshen you come out of an abusive relationship, you are going to have more bad days than good ones. Some days are going to be better than others; however, after some time, you will notice that your emotions will begin to stabilize.

- **Learn to Say No:** Being submissive is a survival mechanism for women in abusive relationships. You would never dare say no to your partner in fear of what might happen. However, now that you are not in an abusive relationship, it is important that you don't carry this submissive nature into your friendships or feel as if you need to say yes to everyone to please them. This will rob you of your energy and time to yourself.

- **Celebrate Your Accomplishments:** No matter how small you think the accomplishment is, celebrate it. Going through a whole day without thinking about your ex is an accomplishment and being consistent with your daily exercise routine is an accomplishment. Pay attention to these things and treat yourself for it.

- **Challenge Yourself:** Is there anything that you have always wanted to do but you have never gotten around to doing it? Make a list of these things and start doing them. You may have always wanted to compete in a triathlon or to get some additional qualifications. Decide that whatever you put your mind to, you are going to achieve.

- **Learn to Trust Yourself:** Before you got into an abusive relationship, your instincts told you that something wasn't right, but you chose to ignore them and pursue the relationship in the hopes that things would get better. Familiarize yourself with that feeling, because any time something isn't right, that is how you will feel, and this isn't just about relationships, it's in all areas of your life.

CHAPTER 14:

DATING AGAIN

L ife does go on after a trauma, and it's essential that you go through all stages of the healing process before you get into another relationship because you don't want to carry any baggage with you. Whether the relationship was abusive or not, people will typically leave one relationship and go straight into another one because they want to fill the void. This is a big mistake. What ends up happening, especially in abusive relationships, is you go from one abusive relationship to the next because that is the energy you are giving off. It's like abusers have some type of radar and they can spot a victim a mile off. However, you can avoid this by taking the time to heal and become a whole person again. When you are confident, and your self-esteem is high, you will attract the right man into your life. Another mistake people make after they have been hurt is avoiding getting into another relationship altogether. There is a big difference between avoiding an abusive relationship and falling in love. Falling in love is a risk. Even if the guy ticks all the boxes, you know he is not a narcissist, and he doesn't have abusive tendencies, you still don't know where the relationship will go. You just have to follow your heart.

The best way to get back onto the dating scene is to start slow; don't rush into things. Here are some tips you can apply to help you move forward in your love life.

- Look out for red flags (we discussed this in chapter 5), listen to your gut instincts, and hit the road if he begins to show any signs of narcissism.

- Keep your options open, don't jump into a relationship with the first man that ticks all the boxes. Spend time dating, get to know a few guys and make sure that you choose the best one.

- Don't make judgments based on your previous relationships. You are dealing with an entirely different person now. If a man feels as if he is being judged based on what someone else did to you, he will be very reluctant to move forward in the relationship. It is important to remember that narcissists are a rare breed; experts believe that only 10% of the population are narcissists, and the percentage is probably higher based on those who haven't been diagnosed. However, when you are bold and full of confidence, it is highly unlikely that you are going to run into a narcissist or any other type of abusive male because they look for a specific type of woman and that isn't you anymore.

- Get a second opinion. A great indicator as to whether a person is a good fit for you is if your friends and family like him. The people closest to you have your best interests at heart—they are capable of seeing things that you might miss. If they like him, move ahead, but if they have compelling reasons why they don't like him, you might need to go back to the drawing board.

- Don't sleep with him until you have both made a serious commitment to each other; sex complicates things. If he is not willing to wait, you know that he is not a keeper.

Remember, regardless of what you were told as a child, or what your former narcissistic partner made you believe, you are awesome, beautiful, vivacious, you have a wonderful destiny, and you have skills and talents to bless people with. You deserve to be loved unconditionally, and one day you will find the relationship of your dreams and live happily ever after!

CHAPTER 15:

FREQUENTLY ASKED QUESTIONS ABOUT NARCISSISTS

There is so much more to say about narcissism that it's impossible to fit it into this book. Therefore, I have included a FAQ section so that I can touch on a few more subjects, even though I am not going into too much depth.

WHAT IS PASSING THE HOT POTATO?

Because narcissists don't like feeling uncomfortable, they use this method to dodge how they are feeling. It's a game they play, and the hot potato is their feelings. Typically, people drop hot potatoes, but in this instance, they pass it along. Someone who likes to feel as if they have everything under control likes to use this method, it's a form of deflection. If you have a narcissistic boss, you will find that he questions everything that you do. They nit-pick, and you start to think that you are incapable of doing anything right. What they are attempting to do is get rid of their feelings of vulnerability by insinuating that you are the one doing everything wrong, when deep down, they feel as if they can't do anything right.

HOW DO I GET AROUND THE HOT POTATO PASS?

By calling it out. You will know how the narcissist is really feeling by the type of questions they ask. This works even better if you're an empath because you will be able to sense their energy and how they are feeling. So, you can say something like, *"Has something happened to make you feel like this today? Something is telling me that you might not be too sure about the project we are working on, or is there something going on with this project that you haven't told me about?"* This will completely disarm the narcissist because they will know they have been called out. At this point, they will either come clean or walk away from the conversation.

WHAT IS THE ONE QUESTION I CAN ASK TO PROVE THAT SOMEONE IS A NARCISSIST?

There are a few questions you can ask, but the type of question that works the best is to ask them about their previous relationships. If they don't take any responsibility for a breakup or feel as if there was nothing they could have done in a relationship to make things better, you know you are dealing with a narcissist. As mentioned throughout this book, narcissists don't take responsibility for anything, they believe that they are always in the right and that they are incapable of doing anything wrong. You probably won't find out the extent of their narcissism from one question, but their answer will give you some insight and you can start probing from there.

WHAT IS STEALTH CONTROL?

Narcissists use this all the time. It is when they engineer circumstances to ensure that they get what they want. Narcissists have a phobia of asking for things directly because they are scared of rejection and it puts them in a position of vulnerability. To avoid this, they will simply make things happen. An example would be your boyfriend turning up at your house with two concert tickets. The concert is literally starting in an hour, you don't even have time to process what's going on, and you are being dragged out of your house to this concert with no preparation or planning. However, when you suggest going to a movie or going out to dinner, your partner is never interested. The reason being is that he wants to have full control over your life and that includes your social activities.

WHAT IS FLUCTUATING EMPATHY?

In the right conditions, narcissists do have the ability to show empathy. Studies have found that when they are prompted to think about a situation from another person's point of view, they are capable of doing so. It is also important to mention that there are some situations where they won't show any empathy, hence the term "fluctuating empathy."

HOW DOES THE TWIN FANTASY WORK?

Basically, it is when the narcissist mirrors the behavior of an empath. When they see that the empath is getting the admiration and the attention that they crave, they immediately go into twin mode and begin to imitate the empath's nature. However, this should never be mistaken as real empathy in that moment—it is their way of getting their narcissistic supply. Narcissists are simply very good at acting.

CONCLUSION

Thank you for taking the time to read this book. Narcissism is a subject that is very dear to my heart and I hope that you now have a deeper understanding of the condition. It is more than just a word we use in casual conversation to describe someone who is full of themselves. Narcissism is a very rare personality disorder that shouldn't be seen in any other way. A person who is slightly unkind or jealous every once in a while is not a narcissist, they're just not having the best of days. This is especially true if they realize that they are in the wrong and they apologize to the person they have hurt or offended for what they have done. However, if the individual does not acknowledge their wrong and believes that their behavior was totally okay, you could have a narcissist on your hands.

Although narcissism is a mental condition that a person has no control over, that doesn't mean you should tolerate their behavior, especially if they are not willing to change and get the help that they need. It isn't easy to get a narcissist out of your life, but it is absolutely necessary if you are ever going to live a fulfilling life.

Narcissism is actually a heart-breaking condition and I wouldn't wish it on my worst enemy. Although it is spoken about in such a negative light because of the damage that it causes other people, we forget to acknowledge the fact that if these people don't get the help that they need, they will end up lonely and depressed for the rest of their lives. What's even sadder is that this is not something that happens often because narcissists don't think that there is anything wrong with them—they truly believe that they are not the ones with the problem.

Even though you have come to the end of this book, if you are currently in a relationship with a narcissist, it's not the end for you and there is still a long way to go in terms of detaching yourself from the situation. So before you go, I want to refresh your memory with these key points:

- A true narcissist must be diagnosed with narcissistic personality disorder (NPD).
- There are fewer female narcissists than there are men.
- Approximately 10% of the population suffer from NPD.
- There are levels of narcissism ranging from mild to severe.
- The main characteristics of a narcissist are delusions of grandeur, an inflated sense of self-importance and a constant desire to be at the forefront of everything. However, these are just some of the most common characteristics, they are many and varied.
- There are categories of narcissists, including toxic, vulnerable, and classic.
- Toxic narcissists are very dangerous and have been closely linked to sociopaths and psychopaths.
- Narcissists are master manipulators, they are highly skilled emotional abusers.
- The majority of narcissists end up alone because they refuse to accept that they have a problem.
- Narcissists are very attracted to empaths, they make an extremely toxic combination.

- The cause of narcissism has never been confirmed; however, there is a possibility that it could stem from childhood, it is also possible that it is genetic.
- Underneath the mask, narcissists are extremely insecure with low self-esteem, they need to be affirmed constantly.
- You cannot change or fix a narcissist; they must see that there is something wrong with them in order for them to go and get the help that they need.
- It can be very difficult to find the strength to leave a narcissistic relationship. Once you do get out, you will need to seek professional help to heal from the emotional abuse you have endured.
- Narcissists use gaslighting to emotionally abuse their victims, it is a very severe and damaging form of abuse that involves manipulating the emotions and thoughts of a person to the extent that they begin to question their own sanity.
- Do not allow a narcissist to make you feel guilty about leaving them, it is essential that you get out of the relationship for your own emotional well-being.

By educating yourself as much as you can on narcissism, you have taken the first steps in the direction to total freedom. Not only will this information assist you in getting out of the relationship you are currently in, but it will ensure that you are never entrapped in this type of partnership again.

I wish you every blessing and success for the future.

THANKS FOR READING!

I really hope you enjoyed this book, and most of all got more value from it than you had to give.

It would mean a lot to me if you left an Amazon review—I will reply to all questions asked!

Simply find this book on Amazon, scroll to the reviews section, and click "Write a customer review".

Or alternatively please visit www.pristinepublish.com/empathnarcissistreview to leave a review.

Be sure to check out my email list, where I am constantly adding tons of value. The best way to currently get on the list is by visiting www.pristinepublish.com and entering your email.

Here I'll provide actionable information that aims to improve your enjoyment of life. I'll update you on my latest books, and I'll even send free e-books that I think you'll find useful.

Kindest regards,

Judy Dyer

ALSO BY
Judy Dyer

Grasp a better understanding of your gift and how you can embrace every part of it so that your life is enriched day by day.

Visit: www.pristinepublish.com/judy

CPSIA information can be obtained
at www.ICGtesting.com
Printed in the USA
BVHW041300171221
624365BV00014B/497

9 781989 588376